PROTOCOLS OF MONEY

Shiv Mehta

Disclaimer Notice:

Please note the information contained within this document is for educational purposes only. All effort has been executed to present accurate, up to date, and reliable, complete information. No warranties of any kind are declared or implied. Readers acknowledge that the author is not engaging in the rendering of legal, financial, or professional advice. Information in this book is in no way intended to replace or supersede financial or any other independent or professional advice. Neither the author nor the publisher may be held responsible for any action or claim resulting from the use of this book or any information contained in it.

ACKNOWLEDGEMENTS

I want to take this opportunity to acknowledge some exceptional people in my life who, over the years, have taught me the true meaning of responsibility. Having a sense of responsibility is one reason behind sharing the knowledge that I have attained with everyone during these testing times we are living post the global pandemic of 2020.

Big thanks to my mom & dad, who always supported me in my independent endeavors to pursue knowledge. My brothers, Suvrat & Sushant, who were my backbone and helped me research the book despite having busy legal careers. My grandparents - Baldev Saigal & Sushil Aneja whose blessings, love, and support remain unconditional. My best friends - Shubham and Abhishek, who not only are always there for me but also provide critical commentary on my work and continuously push me to excel.

A very special thanks to my colleagues, friends, teachers & staff at the University of New South Wales, Sydney - Sheetal Vora, Geoff Briggs, Karen Rodrigues, David Leaney, David Goad, Adam Hinchey, Kevin Brown, David Akers, Kate Virgona, Umesh Banga, Greg Giblett, and Frankie Ryan.

When I landed in New York City to start my MBA at NYU Stern School of Business, I never thought I would complete my MBA journey by having my work published into a book. The book would not have been a reality if not for the support I received from my classmates, friends, and teachers at NYU.

Special thanks to my teachers – Professor Vasant Dhar, Professor Joe Eberhardt, Professor Brett Prescott, Professor Simon Bowmaker and Professor Gary Podorowsky.

The push and encouragement I received from the MBA Class of 2020 for the Blockchain, Digital Currencies & Future of Finance course was heart-warming, with special mention for my friends Joel, Alex, and Emma.

Finally, I am eternally grateful to my Professor of Finance. His passion for teaching the subject of finance and his encouragement to students to use the knowledge attained in economics & finance to better society was inspirational. This book would not have been possible without my teacher and mentor's unwavering support - Professor Ian D'Souza.

FOREWORD

Professor Ian D'Souza
Adjunct Professor of Finance at NYU Stern School of Business

Cryptocurrency is often claimed to be the newest and latest iteration of money. There is rightly a lot of excitement and equally rightly a lot of skepticism associated with this claim. How should cryptocurrencies birth and evolution in the last decade be analyzed in the context of money overall?

In the post-graduate classes I teach on blockchain, digital currencies, and fintech (where Shiv was my student), we purposely begin and end with the history of money. To do this we focus on the core trust dynamics needed for the issuance, acceptance, and exchange of any currency. As the cover of this book illustrates, the currency in which people are willing to place their trust has changed forms, from cows to precious metals to paper to electronic bits. Throughout time, the global reserve currency status has also changed sovereign identity from Rome to Spain to Britain to, currently, the United States.

There is no coincidence that it was (and is) the separation of state and money formation which gave rise, after many iterations, to Bitcoin (the first cryptocurrency, launched during the great financial crisis of 2008-2009). And now a decade later in 2020, with a pandemic, we have seen physical cash and coin circulation collapse and digital native money forms soar in settlement terms.

Bitcoin's money protocol was, amongst many features, its peer-to-peer (P2P) focus, its code-based fixed supply feature, and its mining function, which effectively eliminated the need for human-based audit and, as such, outside third-party authorization. Collectively, these attributes aim to allow money to have no border identity and no region; trust no longer resides with governments or corporations, but within code and between individuals (not institutions).

This transition of trust provides the overarching context of Protocols of Money. Yet as you delve into this text, keep in mind that money protocols are continuously evolving, and many institutions, corporations and governments are now researching a variety of protocol features. No one (cryptographers, computer scientists, economists, lawyers, or bankers) has all the answers. Some are incentivized to maintain authority by preserving the status quo, while others are motivated to take speculative risks, with the hope of a payout via technological advancement. Others face the challenge of even defining terms like "digital assets", "decentralization" and "permissionless". Some of the research avenues you will be introduced to in this book involve mechanizing the transition from paper to electronic currency to reduce "shadow markets," like Central Bank Digital Currencies (CBDC), while others are challenging the very fabric of the sovereign domain of regulatory monetary authorities, enhancing privacy function and censorship dynamics for a new type of global network effect.

To see the energy of the next generation of students, innovators, investors, and users seeking to share cryptocurrencies "value" proposition and challenge notions of it being "made up of thin air" has given this nascent asset class a life force of its own. As part of this new generation, Shiv has diligently consolidated some of these thoughts in the book you are about to read. He will take you on a journey of money protocols, from cows to cryptocurrencies, from regional barter to instant global value transfer. The journey allows us to prepare for the ultimate question: Who will control the "printing presses" of trusted money in the future? Will jurisdictional status quo be maintained (just in a new electronic form) or will a new form of global reserve money—and coded governance—arise? **Protocols of Money** provides us with some initial clues.

Table of Contents

Introduction 1

Chapter 1: **What Is Money?** 3

Chapter 2: **The Evolution of Money** 20

Chapter 3: **History of Capital Markets** 42

Chapter 4: **Major Components of Capital Markets** 47

Chapter 5: **The Great Depression of 1929** 57

Chapter 6: **The Removal of Gold Standard In The 1970s** 70

Chapter 7: **Introduction To Fractional Reserve Banking** 80

Chapter 8: **The Great Recession of 2007** 108

Chapter 9: **The Birth of Bitcoin** 133

Chapter 10: **Evolution of Bitcoin And Cryptocurrencies** 142

Chapter 11: **Birth of Ethereum And Smart Contracts** 180

Chapter 12: **The Great Altcoin Bubble of 2017** 188

Chapter 13: **The Future of Cryptocurrencies Post-2020** 196

References 203

INTRODUCTION

Money substantiates a large portion of our lives, but few people realize what it is. Most of us devote 8-12 hours a day seeking to make money and worry a lot, trying to determine how much we earn to spend or invest.

Though, very few individuals are willing to spend any time reading a book and learn the true meaning of money. Before focusing on Bitcoin, we need to discuss a few key concepts with what money is and a bit of monetary history.

We understand when learning about Bitcoin that this would be a fundamental shift in the way we see money. In short, there have historically been two forms of "money," one focused on a hard commodity like gold, and one focused on a promise, like the euro. Now it appears there's a third kind of money, primarily on math.

The nature of the money we use determines how we behave ourselves against the world and one another. We assume that, for almost all, Bitcoin and digital currencies would have an incredibly beneficial impact.

In this book, we look into the concept of money and its evolution over the years. Also, we examine the birth of bitcoin and the future of cryptocurrencies. We hope that you find this book fascinating, alarming, and empowering.

CHAPTER ONE

WHAT IS MONEY?

The word "money" has several definitions. It is used in our everyday speech, with various connotations. On the one side, when people claim an individual has a ton of money, they generally assume the individual is wealthy. On the other hand, money has a rather particular definition to economists. They see money as something commonly acknowledged in the purchase of goods and services, or debt repayment. It is worthy to note that currency, for example, the euro (€), is one form of capital. However, it would be too restrictive for economists to describe money merely as currency.

According to The Concise Oxford English Dictionary, money is "a current exchange medium known and commonly adopted in goods and services purchases and debt settlement" (The Concise Oxford English Dictionary 12th ed.). One may attach the following to the previous definition: "Money is an established exchange medium in the form of coins and banknotes; money collectively represents coins and banknotes." When it arrives as regular pieces of gold, silver, copper, nickel, etc., marked by government authority and used as a means of trade and measure of interest, it's called hard money; money may be any paper note provided by a government or an approved bank and used in the same way. When it occurs as banknotes (or bills), it is often called paper money.

Money is often used as a form of interest chosen when selling/buying a product of some kind, the price is conventionally measured in a certain amount of units of money; this is the known value of money, agreed by both the vendor and the buyer, as the conventional value may often be used to purchase certain goods, products or services.

A monetary unit chosen as a calculation of worth should not be used extensively. In America, to take one illustration, the British pound reflected the valued norm throughout the colonial era, while the Spanish currency was the mode of trade generally recognized at the time.

Why Money Exists

Money has proved its effectiveness; this is why it still persists in centrally organized economies. The presence of money and its roles as a means of trade and a measure of valuation promote products and services transactions and continuous output specialization. Trade might consist of simple trade of one product for another in a barter-based system, where money was not used, much as primitive cultures used to. It was a very complicated scheme in which the biggest issue is the so-called "double correlation of wanting." For example, a farmer who sells tomatoes in need of a pair of new shoes will not only have to locate a shoemaker who wants to buy tomatoes but also have to reach some form of arrangement as to what the rate of exchange for tomatoes/shoes will be, based on their relative costs. Barter is still practiced worldwide in some places, but nowadays, money is considered a more realistic means of exchange, which facilitates a more substantial amount of economic transactions. In a money economy, it may be exchanged by a manufacturer or the owner of an asset for money, which can be used in additional purchases for commodities and products, thereby avoiding the time and energy taken to locate someone who will consider a barter. Money is viewed as a keystone of daily existence in our current economic society, and this perception is genuinely effective because:

- Money is recognized as Account Unit;
- Appears to be an agreed fundamental way of exchange;
- Conveniently divisible;
- Can be long term and value-stable;

When Did Money Appear?

In Mesopotamia, about 2,500 BC, the very first pieces of information regarding the usage of money appear, and at around the same time, in the ancient kingdom of Lydia. (Several other historical accounts suggest that Chinese coinage emerged in the second millennium B.C.). Money here substituted the barter scheme and decided an actual boom in the variety of goods sold for commercial purposes. Money was introduced mostly from non-economic reasons, including either ancient ceremonial rites and their luxurious, ostentatious ornamentation, or primary modes of barter. Slowly, nature trade increased, and certain items appeared to be picked in comparison to others. This was primarily because of their advantages of being used as exchange media. That is, some were robust and comfortably packed, some were quickly accessible, and had large value densities. Such resources were widely wanted, simple to trade, and recognized as money.

Before the introduction of paper money (i.e., banknotes/Amer. Eng. bills) and coins, early forms of money were used for exchanging products. For example, rice or various small tools in China, cowrie shells in India, cocoa beans in Central America, dog's teeth in Papua New Guinea, quartz pebbles in Ghana or gambling counters in Hong Kong, metal cylinders of different sizes in ancient Asia Minor, metal disks in Tibet, and limestone disks in Yap Islands were the first exchange instruments used as primitive money sources. These items, originally only approved for one-purpose trading operations, slowly proved their growing acceptability and started to be used for other non-economic and general trading purposes, supplementing the barter and eventually effectively replacing it. China is still the most commonly recognized nation as the birthplace of paper currency notes used as money (about 800 AD).

Many ancient societies had their defined codes represented by such rules which were generally agreed by the community, requiring compensation for crime or payment for brides; this was a common tradition, acknowledged rewarding the head of the family for the failure of the services of a spouse. Rulers levied taxes on their people or requested homage from them, and religious leaders often required tribute payments or different types of sacrifice (or offerings). This is how money in ancient societies developed out of profoundly ingrained customs.

From the so-called commodity money, such as rice, cattle and cowrie shells which replaced the earlier exchange of goods method, different types of money have developed: hard money, made of precious metals (especially gold and silver bars and ingots, or coins), token money, made of other metals (e.g., copper), paper money or soft money (also called representative money), such as banknotes (Amer. Eng. bills) forms of replacement money, such as credits and bank deposits, transferable via cheque, treasury bills, or exchange bills, were rapidly pursued.

The latest inventions like the cheque (Amer. Eng. check) and the credit card serve a number, if not any, of the traditional money functions.

FUNCTIONS OF MONEY:

In general words, the main role of money in an economic system is to promote the exchanging of products and services and to assist in the smooth conduct of trade. The essential characteristic is general acceptability. In the following well-known couplet, the roles of money are reflected: "Four A medium, a measure, a standard, a store, money is a matter of functions."

Therefore, money exercises the following four key roles conventionally, each of which overcomes one of the other exchanges of goods difficulty. Exchange medium and value calculations are primary functions because they are of paramount interest, while deferred payment norm and value store are considered secondary functions since they are derived from primary functions.

Money as the Medium of Exchange

"Money came into use to eliminate the inconveniences of bartering because money separated buying from selling" (Singh 2012). The main or primary feature of money is the medium of trade. Through the medium of money, people trade goods and services. Money serves as an exchange medium, or as a form of payment. Money has little worth (except maybe to the miser). It is just an intermediary.

Money use encourages exchange; exchange enables specialization, improves profitability and efficiency. Thus, a healthy monetary structure is of tremendous benefit to human society. Money is often considered a bearer of options or a generalized buying power as it offers freedom of choice to purchase much-needed items from those who give the best bargain.

Money as a Measure of Value or Unit of Account

Money acts as an accounting unit or a value measure. Money is the estimating rod; that is, the units which calculate the prices of certain products and services in terms of money and expressed accordingly. Various goods manufactured in the country are calculated in different units such as cloth meters, milk in liters, and sugar in kilograms.

The exchange of commodities is very complicated without

a specific standard. The values of all products and services can be measured conveniently in a single unit called money. Because, without a calculation of value, there would be no method of pricing. Marketing and development coordinated without a pricing mechanism is not feasible. Therefore, the usage of money as a value indicator is the foundation of advanced output.

The measuring rod of money is important for all modes of economic planning, too. Consumers compare the values of alternative transactions in terms of money. Also, manufacturers compare the costs of alternative transactions in word terms. Producers measure the relative costliness of development variables in terms of value and often schedule their performance depends on the yield of money. Hence, it is incredibly critical that money valuation should remain constant.

Money as the Standard of Deferred Payments

Deferred payments are investments that will be rendered some years later. Usually, debts are represented in terms of account money. Loans are taken out and returned in money terms.

The use of money as the basis of deferred or delayed payments significantly simplifies investing, and lending activities, as capital, typically holds a consistent value over time. Therefore, money promotes capital market development and the role of financial intermediaries such as Stock Exchange, Investment Trust, and Banks. Money is the bridge that connects today's ideals to those of the future.

Money as a Store of Value

For the future, wealth can be stored in money terms. This serves as a liquid store-value for the products. We will get any asset in the future by investing it. Keynes places a lot of focus on the money role. Keeping capital is tantamount to having a reserve of liquid assets because it can quickly be turned into other things.

So, people typically choose to retain some of their wealth in the form of money, as it is challenging to save on goods. Such inclination is regarded as a preference for liquidity. Money is simply the best form of store of value. Wheat or some other product that demands a quantity cannot be retained for an extended period.

These days, another feature, 'Money Liquidity,' is introduced. Money is entirely liquid. Convertibility of cash requires liquidity. Therefore the power to quickly and without loss of interest, turn an asset into capital, is considered asset liquidity. Modern economics put importance on cash liquidity.

Because money is by far the most commonly known asset, it is also the most liquid of all resources. Possession of money allows one to take care of almost every item anywhere, and capital never traps a customer. This is this peculiarity that helps money stand out from all other commodities. A liquidity choice is choice over money.

Money, thus, serves as a shared trade medium, a standard measure of value, a rate of deferred payments, and a store of money.

DIFFERENT APPROACHES OF MONEY

Economists have placed forward a variety of methods for understanding the principle of money. They described the money off concept based on different facets of finance. In past years, though, a controversy has arisen over which elements of money should be included in the money concept.

The numerous money methods can be loosely divided into two categories: the conventional approach and the modern approach.

1. Conventional Approach

The conventional approach is seen as one of the oldest ways of describing money. This just takes into account two aspects of money, namely the medium of trade and value measurement. Consequently, according to this approach, every good or service that fulfills such two roles is called money, irrespective of the fact that money is still a matter of government authentication.

According to this view, cattle (cow, sheep, horse, and bull), grain (wheat, jowar, and rice), stones, and metals (copper, brass, silver, and gold) are commodities that serve the purpose of money. Such products were known as money so long as they fulfilled the two money conditions. Some of the money definitions offered by economists who support the conventional approach are as follows:

According to R.P. Kent, "Money is anything widely used and universally agreed as a medium of trade, or as a value standard."

According to Marshall, "All those things that are (at any time and place) commonly recognized as a way of buying goods and services and defraying expenditures are included in the definition of money without doubt or special examination."

According to Geoffry Crowther, "Money may be described as anything that is commonly agreed as a means of exchange, and at the same time acts as a measure and a store of value."

2. Modern Approach

Over a certain period, it has realized that the conventional approach offers a limiting concept of money. Moreover, money roles are not limited strictly to the medium of exchange and value measurement but include a broad range of functions.

The modern approach to money is widely categorized into three categories; they are as follow:

a. Chicago Approach

Lays focus on expanding the monetary definition provided in the conventional approach. Milton Friedman and his colleagues at the University of Chicago supported the method. Including three more concepts, namely currency, checkable demand deposits, and time deposits, they expanded the description of money provided in the conventional approach.

Economists with conventional money perspectives, however, were opposed to adding the concept time deposit to money definition. Time deposits are not readily available in liquid form or expended directly according to the conventional approach; hence, they do not serve the function of money. The Chicago school of thinking, however, has provided two points illustrating the value of time deposits in identifying money.

These two points are as follows:

I.   Advocated that there is an interrelationship between national income and money, and this interlink may be improved if time deposits are included in the money

II.   Propounded that the concept of money should involve near substitutes of money and time deposit is one of those alternatives

Each of the explications, though, are not good enough to involve time deposits in the money definition.

b. Gurley-Shaw Approach

Includes non-bank financial intermediaries' liabilities when describing money. John G. Gurley and Edward S. Shaw were the main contributors to this approach. When describing the principle of capital, Gurley and Shaw illustrated the relationship of replacement among various factors, such as currency, demand deposits, time deposits, and saving bank deposits.

Those factors serve as the processing value sources. According to Gurley-Shaw, therefore, money may be described as the weighted currency sum, demand deposits, and other deposits and claims against the financial intermediaries. The weights will be allotted based on currency substitutability.

Nevertheless, the realistic consequences of this method are not feasible since the degree of substitutability of deposits and claims against the financial intermediaries is impossible to assess. This is, therefore, a daunting job to assign weights to measure the money supply.

c. Central Bank Approach

This constitutes the broader perspective of the whole money concept. The central bank's function is to control and regulate the money flow within an economy. The central bank then formulates and applies a monetary strategy for achieving its goals and objectives.

To this end, it requires to evaluate all of the origins and methods of payment and credit flow in the economy that are viewed as money. The currency and all other assets which can be translated into money (realizable properties) are included in the money supply according to the central bank view.

United States Radcliffe Committee supported the path adopted by the central bank. According to this body, "the resemblance between currency and other realizable objects or means of transaction to the point that money is dismissed in favor of a wider definition, measurable or immeasurable."

In other words, money can be any form that lends credit to borrowers through. The central bank is introducing numerous measures to control money supply based on monetary policy and policy targets.

TYPES OF MONEY
Commodity Money

This refers to a money form according to the classical approach. Money resources include goods, such as cattle, grains, leather, skins, utensils, and arms. Nevertheless, commodity money is not desirable in the present time because it lacks other essential features of money, such as uniformity, homogeneity, standard size and weight, portability, and divisibility.

Metallic Money

Includes metal money, such as copper, brass, silver, gold, alloys, and aluminum. Because of the limitations of commodity money, the need for metallic money was realized. And the precise date of inventing metallic currency remains unclear.

Metallic coins are thought to have been traded in India around 2500 years ago. The metal parts, such as gold, silver, copper, and aluminum, initially served the role of money. These pieces, however, took the form of coins in later years.

Paper Money

This refers to the money type imprinted, authenticated, and provided by a country's official. Paper money is known to be the most common source of money and is a large part of a country's money supply. Some of the countries have adopted the dual currency note system.

For example, in India, the Reserve Bank of India (R.B.I.) is distributing five rupees notes and coins. R.B.I.'s released currency notes are promissory notes, but they do get legal money status. For example, it is written on every currency note, "I promise to pay the issuer a sum of... Rupees."

Paper money was created as the supply of metallic coins, such as silver and gold, was much smaller than their production. However, a large amount of metallic money is not readily portable, so over time, the value of metallic coins depreciates.

Bank Deposits

It refers to funds in the form of current account deposits, account savings deposits, and time deposits. With the development of the banking system, this type of money was invented. Unlike metallic money and paper money, this source of money for the purchasing of products and services cannot be exchanged hand to hand. Deposit money is used as contributions to the holder's account in the bank's ledger. Only through checks can those deposits be transferred. Money has held some interest since time immemorial; hence, it has demand.

DEMAND FOR MONEY

There is a different demand for money than demand for a commodity. Money demand applies to the sum of money individuals and businesses would have to hold. By contrast, request for a commodity is the demand for the uninterrupted supply of products and services. The significant difference between the demand for service and the demand for money is that the former focuses on the possession, while the latter focuses on the streaming. Earlier, the need for money was known as the amount of money required to make business transactions.

In simple terms, demand for money depended on how many transactions an economy had made. As a result, demand for money was quickly increasing in the boom period, although the demand for oil was declining at the time of stagnation. On the other side, Keynes's modern view of money demand is the form of demand that reflects the need to hold money.

There are three broad reasons why people demand money, which are as follows:

1. Transaction Motive

This refers to the need for money to meet the people's and businesses' existing needs. Individuals need resources to fulfill their current demands, which are considered income motives. On the other side, enterprises need money to carry out their business activities, known as commercial motives. The two money reasons are addressed as follows:

a. Income Motive

This refers to the motives of people who seek money to fulfill their own and family needs. Individuals generally hold cash for bridging the gap between having received income and expenditure.

The income is received once a month, but the spending happens regularly. Therefore, to allow ongoing payments, it is necessary to hold any part of the revenue. The keeping sum depends on the amount of income and the period of income that an individual receives.

b. Business Motive

Refers to corporate demand for money in liquid form to meet current requirements. Businesses need money to procure raw materials, to pay transportation charges, salaries, wages, and other expenditures. The money that companies demand depends on their turnover. The higher turnover indicates the need for a higher amount of money to cover up expenses.

2. Precautionary Motive

This applies to the individuals' desire to keep capital for

various contingencies that may exist in the future. Such eventualities can involve joblessness, illness, and accidents. The sum of money that needs to be held for the precautionary purpose depends on a person's personality and his or her standards of living.

3. Speculative Motive

This refers to individuals' motive to hold cash and benefit from market movements around potential interest rate changes. The precautionary and speculative reason works with different purposes as store of value.

SUPPLY OF MONEY

As discussed above, the demand for money is the demand to hold money. Similarly, money supply applies to the supply of money that will be held. Individuals need to keep the money; otherwise, it does not exist. Money supply relates to the cumulative sum of money (in whatever form) kept by a community for a given period.

In earlier times, the most popular type of money was metallic money, which constituted the central part of money in an economy. Metallic money has been replaced, in modern days, with checkable bank deposits and currency notes.

Money supply is classified into M1, M2, M3, and M4. M1 refers to money stock that comprises coins, currency notes, and deposits on demand. M2 refers to the money stock that includes coins, currency notes, deposits on demand, and deposits on time. M3 refers to the coins, currency notes, demand deposits, time deposits, and post office deposits used in the money stock.

M4 refers to the coins, currency notes, demand deposits, time deposits, post office deposits, savings bank, and term deposits used in the money stock. The credit management policies imposed by a country's banking system help decide the overall money supply.

CHAPTER TWO

THE EVOLUTION OF MONEY

For nearly three thousand years, Money has been a part of human history. This is how the system evolved from the origins of bartering to modern money. At the dawn of human civilization, bartering was used to buy goods instead of money. As the early man began to rear domestic livestock, cattle, sheep, as well as vegetables and grain, were among the earliest forms of bartering. The following are some of the main phases in which money evolved:

- Commodity Money
- Metallic Money
- Paper Money
- Credit Money

- Plastic Money

According to time, place, and circumstances, money has evolved through different stages.

COMMODITY MONEY

We can define commodity money as a physical good that is commonly used by consumers to exchange for specific products. In other terms, it's like the capital we're using now, except it does have a real value. Gold was used as money, for example, but also in jewelry manufacturing. And as a medium of exchange, it had meaning outside of its use.

Any commodity that was generally requested and accepted by common consent was used as money in the earliest period of human civilization. Commonly used as money were goods such as salt, skins, weapons, rice, utensils, wheat, furs, etc. Such exchange of goods for goods was practically called 'Trade by Barter' or 'Barter Exchange.'

Money for commodities is unique in the sense that it is the only form of money that has a fundamental value. Even though we don't use commodities like gold as money anymore, it still has value as jewelry or gilding. We can see, contact, and feel commodity money. This is physical. Moreover, the underlying value makes sure people trust it. What this means is that people can trade it freely in the knowledge that someone will accept it, because it has value in and of itself.

How Commodity Money Originated

The history of product capital goes through millennia and centuries. Indeed, it is virtually impossible to determine its origins accurately. Even so, there are records indicating activity during the 700-500BC period when gold became a common form of money.

Lydian merchants, during this period, produced a gold coin mixed with silver, otherwise known as electrum. They aimed to help improve trading efficiency between countries. It was a useful store of value; it was lasting and universally recognized by nations. Later, it went into full use in 550 B.C., under the order of King Croesus of Lydia.

Not all money made from commodities is the same. Many have been tried and failed because of several factors, but here are some lists of commodity monies used throughout history: Cocoa Beans, Alcohol, Gold, Copper, Salt, Sea Shells, Silver, Tobacco, etc.

Characteristics of Commodity Money
1. Durable

Commodities such as meat would not be useful as they go bad over time. Similarly, metals like iron would not be enough because it easily rusts. If the commodity is unable to retain its intrinsic value, then the confidence therein begins to diminish.

2. Divisible/Measurable

We have to have a particular way of measuring money. The development of metric units such as ounces and pounds has paved the way for these. As a result, we are willing to buy various goods at different prices. If we can't measure money, we can't measure how much we're prepared to pay. If there was only one $50 note in circulation, this makes buying something at $1 incredibly difficult.

3. Easily Exchangeable

No-one wants the hassle of marketing a cow. Using gold coins that are much lighter and easier to carry is much more convenient.

4. Rarity

It is a commodity money in that the supply is limited must be rare. Nevertheless, the money supply still has to be able to respond to rising economic output. This is to say the product supply must be able to respond to growing demand. And as the economy starts to grow, the commodity must be in a place to support and serve the new products in the market.

How Commodity Money Has Gained Widespread Use

Commodity money has what is perceived as an 'intrinsic value' in economic terms. That means it has a value that goes beyond its use as money. So anything that has an alternative usage could be considered a form of money commodity.

Commodity's 'intrinsic value' is a crucial part in building its trust. We can look back to when goods like tobacco or salt were used as money for many centuries. People would use tobacco and salt as commodities commonly used to trade with each other. Even if nobody would accept it, the owner could use it for their purposes. And if anyone is trying to sell a pound of tobacco and nobody would consider it, they could smoke it instead. Through the years, trust in commodities gradually developed. Although traders may not accept it, the population was left reassured that it had alternative uses.

Part of the faith in commodity money often derives from its rareness, or at least how people view its uniqueness. Commodities like gold are, of course, rare. It is because of this rarity that the commodity becomes more valuable, and its intrinsic value increases. By contrast, we do have product monies such as salt and tobacco. The scarcity of these resources depends mostly on its use and creation. In other terms, how to restrain supply.

Such commodities had not been very successful. There was an aspect of trust in them, though. This is because the supply had been self-regulating for a time. In addition to this, farmers might grow vast amounts of tobacco; however, the population would not consume in equal proportions. Nevertheless, there was a fundamental issue in the fact that supply would ultimately outstrip demand, meaning an abundant amount of tobacco or salt was present. This inevitably led to inflation, as it was a form of money.

FROM COMMODITY MONEY TO METALLIC MONEY

As human civilization progressed, commodity money changed into metallic money. Metals such as copper, silver, gold, etc. have been used, because they can be accurately handled and can be easily measured in quantity. It was the primary type of money in the most significant portion of the history documented.

Throughout history, metals were used as money. According to Aristotle's observation, the various necessities of life are not easily carried out; hence, in their dealings with each other, people agreed to employ something that was intrinsically useful and easily applicable to life's purposes — for example, iron, silver, etc. At first, the metal's value was measured by weight, but in time governments or sovereigns put a stamp on it to avoid the difficulty of weighing it and to make the value known in sight.

The practice of using metal as money can be dated back to Babylon more than 2000 years B.C., but until the 7th-century, standardization and certification in the form of coinage took place in B.C. era except perhaps in isolated instances. Historians generally ascribe Croesus, King of Lydia, a state in Anatolia, to the first use of coined money. Made of electrum, a natural mixture of gold and silver, the earliest coins were crude, bean-shaped ingots with a primitive punch mark certifying either weight or fineness or both.

The use of coins allowed payment to be by "tale," or count, rather than weight, which greatly facilitated commerce. But this, in turn, urged "clipping" (shaving off tiny slivers from the sides or edges of the coins) and "sweating" (shaking a bunch of coins together in a leather bag and thus collecting the knocked off dust) in the hope of passing on the lighter coin at its face value. Gresham's law described the resulting economic situation (that "bad money drives out good" when there is a fixed exchange rate between them): heavy and good coins were kept for their metallic importance and value, while light coins were passed on to others. With time, the coins grew lighter and lighter, and higher and higher prices.

For large transactions, payment by weight would be revived as a way to correct this problem, and pressure for recovery would be exerted. Coin's milling (serrations across a coin's circumference), which started in the late 17th century, mostly ended these particular defects.

A more severe issue arose when the sovereign attempted to take benefit of the monopoly of coinage. The Greek and Roman experiences offer an interesting contrast in this respect. Solon had introduced a partial currency debasement after taking office in Athens in 594 BC. The Athenian drachma had an almost constant silver content (67 grains of fine silver before Alexander, 65 grains later) for the next four centuries (before Greece was incorporated into the Roman Empire); and became the standard coin of commerce in Greece, as well as in much of Asia and Europe. In around the 2nd century B.C., well after the Roman invasion of the Mediterranean peninsula, the drachma began to be minted and extensively used.

The Roman experience was very different. Not long after the silver denarius, modeled after the Greek drachma, was introduced about 212 BC, the previous coinage of copper (libra) began to be debased until its weight had been reduced by the beginning of the empire, from 1 pound (about 450 grams) to half an ounce (about 15 grams). By comparison, the silver denarius and the gold aureus (introduced roughly 87 B.C.) endured only slight debasement before Nero's time (A.D. 54), when almost constant coinage tampering started. The metal content of the silver coins and gold has been reduced, while the alloy ratio has been increased to three-fourths or more of its mass. Debasement in Rome (as ever since) exploited the income of the state from money creation to cover its inadequacy or inability to fund its expenditure by specific taxes. But the debasement in effect raised prices exacerbating the economic situation in Rome which led to the empire's collapse.

Metallic money was introduced to overcome the problems associated with using commodity money. The coins were allegedly minted in Goddess Juno's temple. This is why they recognized the coins as money. Metallic money has two types. They are as follows:

Standard metallic money:

This is metallic money made of pure and superior metals such as gold and silver. The face value of this kind of metallic money is just equal to the intrinsic value. The value inscribed in the coins is called Money face value. The metal value used for coin minting is called the intrinsic value.

Token money:

It is metallic money, which consists of impure and inferior metals. This kind of metallic money has a face value higher than the value intrinsic to it. Since, with time, the prices of metals change, the standard metallic money is not the correct type of money. Also, large amounts of superior and pure metals are needed to mint the large quantity of the coins. In fact, metallic money is uniform and lasting. This is hard to bring in significant amounts. There is also a problem with metal scarcity to mint the coins.

PAPER MONEY

Paper money is the official paper currency of a nation used for the transactions used in the purchase of products and services. To keep the flow of funds in line with monetary policy, the printing of paper money is typically regulated by a central bank or treasury of a country. Paper money tends to be updated with new versions containing security features, including efforts to render illegal copies more difficult for counterfeiters.

The first recorded use of paper money during the 7th century A.D. was presumed to be in the country of China. To reduce the need to carry heavy and weighty strings of metallic coins to conduct transactions. Individuals would transfer their coins to a trustworthy party, similar to making a deposit at a modern bank, and then receive a note denoting how much money they had deposited. The note could then be rescheduled at a later date for currency.

Experience had shown that it was difficult and threatened failure or theft to hold vast amounts of gold, silver, or other metals. More than 1,000 years ago, in China, the first use of paper money happened. In the 18th and 19th centuries, paper money and banknotes had developed across the globe. The bulk of the funds in usage originated not from real gold or silver but fiduciary assets — promises to pay specified gold and silver sums. Initially, these promises were issued by individuals or firms as banknotes or as transferable book entries, which came to be called deposits. Although deposits and banknotes began on deposit at a bank or with a merchant as claims for gold or silver, this later changed. The banker (or merchant) may issue more gold and silver claims than the sum in the safekeeping, knowing that everyone would not claim their balance at once. Bankers will either be willing to spend the difference or loan it at interest. However, in times of trouble, the banks may fail when borrowers did not repay their loans or in the case of over-issue.

Governments gradually took on supervisory role. They

specified legal tender, defining the type of payment which, when offered to the creditor, legally discharged debt and could be used to pay tax. The weight and metallic composition of the coins are also set by governments. They consequently replaced fiduciary paper money — promises to pay in gold or silver — with fiat paper money — that is, notes issued on the sovereign government's "fiat," are specified as so many dollars, pounds, or yen, etc., and are legal tendering but are not promises to pay anything else.

In the early 18th century, France sponsored the first large-scale issue of paper money in a Western country. From 1789 to 1796, the French Revolutionary Government then issued tasks. Similarly, the American colonies, and then the Continental Congress, released credit bills that could be used to make payments. Yet those and other early experiments gave a deservedly lousy name to fiat money. The money was over-issued, and prices rose significantly until the money became worthless or was redeemed to a small fraction of its initial value in metallic money (or promises to pay metallic money).

Subsequent issues of fiat money during the 19th century were temporary departures from a metallic standard in the major countries. In Great Britain, for example, during the Napoleonic Wars (1797–1815), the government suspended payment of gold for all outstanding banknotes. The Government has issued fiat paper money to finance the war. As a result, prices in Great Britain doubled, and gold coin and bullion in paper terms became more expensive. The Government deflated the price ratio by growing the volume of money to restore the gold standard at the former gold price. Great Britain reclaimed the gold standard in 1821.

Similarly, the U.S. government suspended convertibility of Union currency (greenbacks) into specie (gold or silver coin) during the American Civil War, and resumption did not occur until 1879 (see Specie Payment). At its peak in 1864, gold's greenback worth, nominally equal to $100, had hit over $250.

These episodes, which have been replicated in other nations, have taught the public that war is bringing inflation and that the result of war is bringing deflation and depression. That is not an inevitable sequence. It mirrored the experience of the 19th century under metallic money standards. Wars usually involved heightened government spending and budget deficits. The metallic (gold) standard was abolished by governments and their shortcomings funded by investing and printing paper money. Prices went up.

Throughout history, when wartime spending and inflation ended, the price of gold would be well above its pre-war value. Prices quoted in paper money had to fall to restore the metallic standard to the pre-war price of gold in paper money. The alternative was to accept the higher price of gold in paper money by devaluing the currency (that is, reducing the buying power of money). The British and U.S. governments forced down prices after World War I, but many other countries devalued their currencies against gold. All the major countries accepted the higher wartime price level after World War II, and most devalued their currencies to avoid deflation and depression.

Many issues brought by the widespread use of paper money. Because the value of producing paper money is significantly lower than its exchange value, forgery is common (it cost about 4 cents in 1999 to create one piece of U.S. paper money). Later, the development of copying machines required changes in paper and the use of metallic strips and other devices to exacerbate forgery. The usage of computers to identify, count, or change currency has increased the need for checks to recognize real currency.

There are two kinds of money on paper. They are: reversible Paper Money and Inconvertible. Paper money has come to occupy an essential place in almost all countries of the world's modern monetary system. The term paper money applies only to government notes and notices issued by the country's central bank. The issuing authority backed them in the early times when notes were introduced by an exactly equal amount of gold or silver kept in reserve.

When required, such notes could be exchanged for gold or silver coins, and did nothing but represent metallic coins. Therefore, such paper money or notes are called representative paper money. Nowadays, paper money isn't entirely protected by gold or silver. Representative paper money is not to be seen in the world.

Convertible Paper Money

"Paper money stayed as convertible paper money for a long time. Money under this is convertible into regular gold or silver coins. Under it, the paper currency issued by the Central Bank was fully supported by its equal value reserves of gold and silver" (Supriya 2013).

This paper currency system was therefore called "Full Reserve System." Still, over time it was felt that a reserve of one hundred percent against the issued paper money was not required, and instead, only a proportion of 30 to 50% was necessary to convert the notes offered for conversion to gold.

Hence, the adoption of a proportional reserve system. Accordingly, the issuing authority has been called upon to retain a 30 to 50% of the total amount of notes issued as gold reserves. When they were present for exchange into gold, a percentage of 30 to 50 was considered sufficient to honor the notes. It was based on the fact that people found notes very convenient, and they rarely thought they were presented to the issuing authority. Full backup of gold was therefore not required. This proportional reserve system was adopted in India in 1927 and continued until 1957.

Inconvertible Paper Money

Money is not convertible into gold or other precious metals under the inconvertible paper money system. So, when paper money is inconvertible, it is not the responsibility of the issuing authority to convert the paper notes into gold or gold coins. The currency notes issued by almost all the central banks of the world currently are fiat paper money; that is, they are issued by the government's fiat, i.e., order).

They are usually appropriate because they are legal tender in exchange for products and services and debt payment. This should be remembered that on the currency notes written, 'promises to pay' are not 'promises to compensate' anything else. Only other paper notes will be issued for such notes whose worth will be equivalent to the face value of the note that you are present for payment.

Credit Money

Credit money is the monetary value generated by a potential bond or claim. As such, credit money arises out of credit extension or debt issuance. In the modern fractional reserve banking system, commercial banks can create credit money by issuing loans in higher amounts than the reserves which they hold in their vaults.

Other types of credit money exist, such as I.O.U.s, bonds, and money markets. Virtually any kind of financial instrument which cannot or is not expected to be repaid immediately may be viewed as credit money.

The payment money practically existed side by side with that of paper profits. People hold some of their cash as bank deposits, which can be withdrawn by checks at their convenience. The cheque itself (also known as credit money or bank money) is not property but serves the same functions as money.

According to recent research in economic history, anthropology, and sociology, scholars now believe credit was the first form of money that preceded paper money coin. Many of the earliest writings discovered in ancient times have been translated as tallies of debts owed by one group to another-before the discovery of money itself. This form of value obligation, for example, I owe you X-is mostly credit money as soon as it is possible to transfer that obligation to someone else in kind. I may owe you X, for example, but you can pass your claim against me to your brother because I owe your brother X now. You and your brother were practically making credit money transactions.

During the crusades of the Middle Ages, the Roman Catholic Church's Knights Templar, a religious group powerfully armed and committed to holy war, kept valuables and commodities in trust. This led to the creation of a modern system of credit account, which is still prevalent today. Over the years, public trust in credit money institutions waxed and waned, depending on economic, political, and social factors.

PLASTIC MONEY

Plastic money is a term used instead of real banknotes to describe the rough plastic cards used in day to day life. They come in several types, including debit cards, credit cards, store cards, and prepaid cash cards. After 1970, when the specific standards for a magnetic strip were set, the plastic cards began to be widely used. The credit card concept was introduced in India in 1981 and was on the verge of an exceptional boom.

Today the domestic card industry is applied with various types of gold, silver, global, smart to secure, co-branded credit cards, etc. There's vast potential for growth in the domestic card industry.

Types of Plastic of Money
Charge Card

A Charge Card has similar credit card features. However, it is necessary to pay the entire amount of bill until the due date, after using a charge card. If the individual defaults to pay the charge card cost, then the late payment penalties must be charged.

MasterCard & Visa

Visa & MasterCard are for-profit international organizations. They're dedicated to fostering the growth of card business worldwide. They have designed a wide network of merchant institutions to facilitate multiple transactions worldwide.

Debit Cards

The debit card is an encoded plastic card issued by banks that has been replaced by the cheques. It allows the customers to pay without carrying cash in exchange for goods and services. It is a multipurpose card since it can be used at an A.T.M. to withdraw money and check the bank account balance. It is issued with the savings or the current account free of cost by bank. It is one of the best online payment tools in which the purchase amount is immediately subtracted from the client's account and credited to the merchant's account. It surmounted the delay in the payment process. There are currently two ways in which transactions with debit cards are processed: On-line debit (also called P.I.N.) and Offline debit (also called signature debit)

A.T.M. Cards

Usually, these cards are used in A.T.M.s to withdraw money, move funds, and create deposits. For security purposes, A.T.M. cards are used by inserting the card into a machine and entering a P.I.N. or a personal number. Before making any transaction, the system checks the account for sufficient funds.

Plastic Money History

You can't ignore charge cards with a "plastic money"

history. Charge cards established the basis for debit and credit cards. You can find charging cards issued by companies as far back as the early 1900s. Majorly, these cards just kept customers loyal to the company.

1900-1950s CARDS
Charg-it

The first actual bank card was "Charg-it" and was issued in 1946. A banker in Brooklyn invented the card, by the name of John Biggins. However, that could only be achieved on local purchases.

The Diners Club Card

Frank Mcnamara initially took up the credit card concept. Frank found himself short of cash during dinner with a fellow business associate when he lost his wallet. What followed was an epiphany, which led him to consider a charge card. This card, later referred to as the "Diners Club Card," could be used at multiple locations. This novel idea became the first exact Multi-purpose Charging Card model.

American Express

In 1958 American Express issued its first credit card. The Green Charge Card was approved globally, owing to its international reach. It was the first credit card and was available internationally.

BankAmericard

Bank of America introduced a unique card in 1958 that could be used at participating merchants to buy anything. This was a universal card, in other words, so that the cardholder did not need multiple cards for specific destinations. This card also sets industry standards, including grace periods of 25 days, credit limits, and floor limits. Initially, the pilot program had 60,000 clients in 1959, which became a big hit. In California, the program was then rolled out state-wide.

1960s CARDS
The Mag Stripe

Without the Mag tag, credit and debit cards wouldn't be what they are now. This momentous leap in card technology came when the C.I.A. hired I.B.M. to attach its identity cards to a magnetic stripe. The technology was already available; however, the main problem was that the stripe was permanently attached to the card without wrinkles. Forest Perry came home from work to find his wife ironing her clothes while working on this problem. When he mentioned the stripe problem, Forest's wife asked for a look at the prototype card. Using the iron, she managed to wrinkle-free melt the stripe to the coin. This solved the whole problem, which enabled I.B.M. to go into full production on all their cards with the Mag Stripe.

Automated Teller Machine (A.T.M.)

All-serving A.T.M. is one of the most convenient aspects of plastic money. John Shepperd-Barron brought the A.T.M. (Automated Teller Machine) into existence in the 1960s. John had to wait for the next day following an unexpected and disappointing ride to the store before it opened again. That night John was thinking of a self-dispensing cash machine while he was reportedly taking a bath. He also invented the 4-digit international standard pin code, along with the invention of what was soon to become the A.T.M. John initially requested a six-digit serial for the army. Still, his wife persuaded him that it would be better to recall four digits.

The Chicago Debacle

Unsolicited credit cards became a significant problem for the Chicago market during the 1960s. By the mid-60s, the demand in Chicago was untapped by credit card firms, so many businesses began mailing "pre-approved tickets." For those credit card companies, this mailing tactic proved to be almost fatal, because they accidentally sent them to convicted felons, kids and even dogs. It also took advantage of organized crime rings by using corrupt workers to intercept cards. Because these intercepted cards had already been pre-approved, the people residing at the mailing address billed thousands of dollars without even knowing about the stolen cards.

1970s –1990s CARDS
VISA

The Visa card originally started as the BankAmericard program and was never intended to go nationally or internationally in this respect. BankAmerica began to a licensing program with banks located around California in 1965. BankAmerica was able to create a joint venture bank association after enough banks signed up to the program. This eventually unfolded on an international scale, and BankAmerica changed its card name to VISA International. They also created a domestic version of America named VISA U.S.A. This two-card system made it easier for VISA International to be accepted in other countries because it had no association with America. The acronym VISA stands for Visa International Service Association; BankAmerica felt the change of name was appropriate as VISA would be recognized instantly in many different languages. They continued their success and eventually joined the Plus A.T.M. network becoming even more accessible to customers around the world. Such strategic choices in branding helped VISA to become one of today's most recognized and successful consumer brands.

Mastercard

While the BankAmericard gained precedence across California, they also gained substantial ground in their competition at Kentucky. In 1966, Crocker National Bank, Wells Fargo, and Bank of California joined forces and launched the Interbank Card Association (I.C.A.). Mastercharge changed its logo three years later and came out with the iconic red and overlapping orange circle. It wasn't until ten years later though that Mastercharge became the Mastercard we know today. For MasterCard, the 80s was also a revolutionary decade. They released their program to replace their emergency cards; they entered the Pacific Rim and acquired Cirrus, the world's largest A.T.M. network. MasterCard capitalized on their developments after such a productive decade and, along with VISA, became the other key player on the market.

Discover Card

In the 1980s, the Discover Card was a revolutionary card. It specifically featured a new credit card option for Sears and Roebuck & Co. customers. This card has been the first of its type to have no annual fee, cashback, and small credit limitations. The only problem was that since it was linked to Sears, other retailers were tired of accepting it because they would help their competition. Eventually, Discover noticed that their brand had to differentiate entirely from Sears and so they proceeded. Separating from Sears made Discover more attractive for the card to be adopted by other merchants. Discover was incredibly successful by the early 1990s and was known as a merit rival to Visa and MasterCard.

1990s–Today

Credit and debit cards have become more efficient and instantly accessible across multiple media to blend into an ever-evolving technological world. This poses various possibilities for retailers and customers alike, with new technologies such as mobile platforms.

Chip and Pin

The adoption of chip and pin technologies came with one of the most revolutionary adjustments to plastic money. This device has become a credit and debit card standard, which is compared to the magnetic stripe. Chip and Pin technology makes cards far more secure, and because of the encrypted chip, personal information is complicated to steal. A cloned chip can also be recognized immediately as a fraudulent card since each chip is encrypted specifically for each card. Although this card technology has been around since the 1990s, it has become used nationally across Canada and became compulsory in the U.S. from October 1, 2015.

Square

A game-changer for businesses is being able to allow transactions through a mobile app. This was made possible in large part by a company called Square. Square allowed the use of a cell phone as a point-of-sale system and accepted card payments wherever possible. The device simply plugs into the headphone jack, so the user has a card slot to swipe their card. Mobile card readers have definitely made a significant contribution to plastic money introduced to the market with a flat-rate fee of 2.75%. Square has opened the door for many small businesses across the globe who can now offer more ways to pay their consumers.

Bling Tag

The Bling Tag makes paying over mobile devices even faster. It is a sticker that usually contains a chip called N.F.C. (Near Field Communication). The N.F.C. chip is using the same technology as your traditional debit or credit card. Just like taping a credit or debit card, any Bling Tag user only needs to press their handset on the acceptor pad. This is comfort on a whole new level. Consumers are allowed to leave their wallets or purses at home.

CHAPTER THREE

HISTORY OF CAPITAL MARKETS

What is Capital Market?

Capital markets are a market for buyers and sellers in financial securities such as bonds, stocks, and so on. Participants such as individuals and institutions undertake in the buying/selling. Capital markets are helping to channel surplus funds from savers to institutions that then invest in productive use. This market generally deals in long-term securities.

Capital markets are composed of the main and secondary markets. Primary markets deal with trade in new stock issues and other securities, while the secondary market deals with the exchange of existing securities or previously issued ones. Another important division in the capital market is made based upon the nature of the traded security, i.e., the stock and bond market.

Modern capital markets are almost always operated on computer-based electronic trading platforms; most can only be used via financial sector agencies or government and corporate treasury departments, but some can be viewed directly by the public. For example, an American citizen with an internet connection in the United States can create an account with TreasuryDirect and use it to buy bonds in the primary market. However, sales to individuals constitute only a tiny fraction of the total volume of bonds sold. Several private firms provide browser-based platforms that enable individuals to purchase shares and sometimes even bonds in secondary markets. There are several thousands of such systems, most of which cover only limited sections of the capital markets at large. Entities that host the programs include stock exchanges, investment banks, and departments of government. The systems are physically hosted all over the world, although they tend to be concentrated in financial centers such as London, New York, and Hong Kong.

THE HISTORY

The Dutch became the first to utilize a fully-fledged capital market (including the bond and stock market) adequately to fund companies (such as the Dutch East India Company and the Dutch West India Company). While the Italian city-states produced formal bond markets for the first time, they did not develop the other ingredient needed to create a full capital market: the formal stock market.

It was in the Dutch Republic of the 17th century that the global securities market was beginning to assume its modern form. The Dutch East India Company (V.O.C.) became the first company to bid stock shares. Over the 200-year existence of the Organization, the dividend was about 18% of income. The V.O.C.'s launch of the Amsterdam Stock Exchange (a.k.a. Beurs van Hendrick de Keyser in Dutch) in the early 1600s has long been regarded as the root of 'ordinary' stock exchanges dealing in securities (such as bonds and common shares) sold by corporations establishing and sustaining secondary markets.

The first set of people to trade their shares on a regular stock exchange were the Dutch. The buying and selling of these equity options in the V.O.C. was the basis of the first legal (formal) stock market in existence. The old methods of stock-market manipulation had been developed in the Dutch Republic. The Netherlands pioneered stock futures, stock options, short sell, bear raids, debt-equity swaps, and other speculative techniques.

CAPITAL MARKET CLASSIFICATION
Primary Market

The primary market is a new issue market; it deals exclusively with problems involving new securities. It is the location where first-time stock trading is done. The main objective is capital formation, also known as Initial Public Offer (I.P.O.) for government, institutions, companies, etc. Now let's take a peek at primary market functions:

- Origination: It is referred to as the examination, evaluation, and processing of new project proposals in the primary market. It begins until an issue is present on the market. It is done with the help of commercial bankers.

- Underwriting: There is a need for underwriting firms to ensure the success of a new issue. They are the ones that secure minimum subscription.
- Distribution: Brokers and dealers take up the job of distribution, and they are to reach out to the investors directly.

Secondary Market

The secondary market is a location where private shares are traded in. This is classified as stock exchange or capital exchange. Here the investors buy the securities and sell them. Now let's take a look at secondary market functions:

- Regular information regarding safety value;
- Offers investors liquidity for their assets;
- Continuous & active trading;
- Build a marketplace

FUNCTIONS OF CAPITAL MARKET

- Strengthens economic growth
- It helps to connect investors with savers
- Mobilization of savings for long-term investment finance
- Facilitates the movement of capital to make more profits and to boost national income productively
- Quick valuations of financial instruments
- Fosters securities trading

- Reduces transaction and the use of information
- It offers insurance against market or price threats through derivative trading
- Enhancement of the capital allocation efficiency
- Fosters a broad spectrum of productive asset ownership
- Maintains funds availability
- Enables settling of transactions

CHAPTER FOUR

MAJOR COMPONENTS OF CAPITAL MARKETS

International Equity Markets

Companies sell their stake of financial markets. Global equity markets are all stocks traded outside the country of origin of the issuing company. Most big global firms aim to take advantage of the global financial hubs and issue stocks in major markets to finance local and regional operations.

ArcelorMittal, for example, is a global steel company headquartered in Luxembourg; it is listed on the Bilbao, New York, Paris, Amsterdam, Luxembourg, Madrid, Brussels,

Barcelona, and Valencia stock markets. Although the daily value of global stocks varies, the international equity markets have expanded significantly in the past decade, giving global firms increased opportunities to fund their global operations. The critical factors for the growth in the international equity markets are:

- Growth of Developing Economies. As developing countries grow, their domestic firms seek to expand into global markets and take advantage of more flexible and cheaper financial markets.
- Propel privatization. The general trend in developing and emerging markets over the last two decades has been to privatize state-owned enterprises predominantly. These entities tend to be significant, and it infuses trillions of dollars of new equity into local and global markets when they sell some or all of their shares. Such shares are bought by domestic and global investors who are keen to engage in regional economic growth.
- Investment banks. Investment banks also lead the way in growing global stock markets with increased opportunities in new emerging markets and the desire to quickly expand their businesses. Such specialized banks tend to be retained by major firms in developed countries or governments seeking privatization to issue and sell the stocks outside the local nation to investors with deep pockets.
- Advancements in technology. Expansion of technology into global finance has opened up new opportunities for investors and firms around the world. Technology and

the Internet have provided better and cheaper ways to trade stocks and, in some cases, smaller firms issuing shares.

International/Foreign Bond Markets

Landbuckets.org asserts that "bonds are the most common form of debt instrument, which is essentially a loan from the holder to the bond's issuer" (Landbucket.org). The international bond market is composed of all the bonds sold outside their home country by an issuing company, government, or entity. Companies that do not wish to issue more equity shares and dilute existing shareholder ownership interests prefer to use bonds or debt to raise capital (i.e., money). For a variety of reasons, companies could access the international bond markets, including funding a new production facility or expanding their operations in one or more countries. There are several types of foreign bonds, detailed in the sections that follow.

Foreign Bond

A foreign bond is a bond sold in another country by a company, government, or entity and issued in the currency of the country it is being sold in. Foreign bonds are associated with foreign exchange, economic, and political risks, and many sophisticated buyers and issuers of these bonds use complex hedging strategies to reduce the risks. For example, the yen-denominated bonds issued by global corporations in Japan are called Samurai bonds. There are other names to similar bond structures, as you might expect. Foreign bonds sold in the U.S. and denominated in U.S. dollars are referred to as Yankee Bonds. In the U.K., these international bonds are referred to as bulldog bonds. Foreign bonds issued and traded across Asia except Japan are referred to as dragon bonds, typically denominated in U.S. dollars. Foreign bonds in the country in which they are issued are generally subject to the same rules and guidelines as domestic bonds. Regulatory and reporting requirements also exist, which makes them a slightly more expensive bond than the Eurobond. The requirements add small costs that other businesses will rack up considering the scale of the bond issues.

Eurobond

A Eurobond is a bond issued outside of the country where it is denominated in currency. Eurobonds are not regulated by the governments of the countries in which they are issued, and thus the most popular form of international bond is Eurobonds. An example of a Eurobond is a debt issued by a Japanese corporation, denominated in U.S. dollars, and sold only in the U.K. and France.

Global Bond

A global bond is a bond that's sold in several global financial centers simultaneously. It is denominated usually in U.S. dollars or Euros. By simultaneously offering the bond in several markets, the firm will raise the costs of issuing it. Usually, this option is reserved for higher-rated, creditworthy, and typically huge companies.

Eurocurrency Markets

The Eurocurrency markets emerged in the 1950s when communist governments in Eastern Europe were worried that, for political purposes, the U.S. government could confiscate or obstruct any deposits of its dollars in U.S. banks. By depositing their dollars into European banks that would hold dollar accounts for them, these communist governments addressed their concerns. This produced what is known as the Eurodollar - U.S. dollars deposited in European banks. Banks in other countries, including Japan and Canada, have been around for years, have also begun keeping deposits from U.S. dollars, and now Eurodollars are any dollar deposits in a bank outside the US. (The Euro- prefix is still just a historical reference to its early days.) The Eurodollar extension is the Eurocurrency, which is a currency on deposit in the country of issue. Although Eurocurrencies can be in any denominations, nearly half of world deposits are in Eurodollars.

Also, the Euroloan market is an increasing part of the Eurocurrency market. The Euroloan sector is one of the least costly for huge, creditworthy borrowers, including governments and big global corporations. Euroloans are quoted on the basis of LIBOR, the London Interbank Offer Rate, which is the interest rate on short-term Eurocurrency loans that banks in London charge each other.

The Eurocurrency market's most significant appeal is that there are no regulations that lead to lower costs. The Eurocurrency market participants are huge global businesses, banks, governments, and highly wealthy individuals. As a result, the transaction sizes tend to be large, providing lower transaction costs for an economy of scale and networks overall. The Eurocurrency markets are relatively inexpensive, short-term financing solutions for Eurocurrency loans; they are also a short-term investing choice for Eurocurrency depositing entities with excess funds.

Offshore Centers

The world's first levels of centers are the world's financial centers, which are basically central business and finance points. They are usually home to major corporations and banks, or to global firms at least regional headquarters. They do have at least one stock exchange and is involved globally. While both the ranking format and the year may differ in their actual order of importance, the following cities rank as global financial centers: New York, London, Tokyo, Hong Kong, Singapore, Chicago, Zurich, Geneva, and Sydney.

Besides the global financial centers, there is a group of countries and territories that comprise offshore financial centers. An offshore financial center is a country or region with few rules governing the entire financial sector and low overall taxes. As a result, it is considered tax havens for many offshore centers. Many of these countries or regions are socially and economically secure, so in most instances, the local government has decided that it is their primary industry to be an offshore financial center. As a result, they invest in technology and infrastructure in the international financial marketplace to remain globally linked and competitive.

Types of well-known overseas financial hubs include the Cayman Islands, Bahamas, Panama, British Virgin Islands, Anguilla, Bermuda and Barbados. They appear to be small countries or regions, so although multinational companies do not base any of their activities at such sites, they often integrate into these offshore centers to circumvent the higher taxes they will have to pay in their home countries and to take advantage of the efficiencies of such financial centers. For the same benefits, many global firms can house financing subsidiaries in offshore centers. For starters, the spirits manufacturer Bacardi has sales of $6 billion, more than 6,000 workers worldwide, and twenty-seven global production plants. The business is headquartered in Bermuda, enabling it to take advantage of the lower tax levels and financial efficiencies to manage its global operations.

Because of the size of financial transactions flowing through these offshore centers, they have become extremely relevant to the global capital markets.

Investment Banks, International Banks, Global Financial Firms, and Securities Firms, Roles

Over the last few decades, the role of international banks, investment banks, and securities firms has evolved. Let's have a look at each of these institutions' primary purpose and how it has changed, as several have combined to become global financial powerhouses.

International banks have historically expanded their domestic role to the global arena by serving the needs of multinational companies (MNC). Such banks not only received deposits and made loans but also supported export and import finance tools and offered sophisticated cash management tools like foreign exchange. For example, a business that buys goods from another country may require short-term acquisition financing, transfers of electronic funds (also called wires), and foreign exchange transactions. All these services are supported by international banks, and more.

There are different types of banks in broad strokes, and based on their activities, they may be divided into several groups. Retail banks deal directly with customers and typically concentrate on products from the mainstream industry, such as checking and saving accounts, mortgages and other loans, and credit cards. Private banks, on the other hand, usually provide wealth-management services to high net worth families and individuals. Business banks provide services to medium-sized enterprises and other organizations, whereas corporate bank clients are typically major business entities. Finally, investment banks offer financial-market facilities, such as mergers and acquisitions. Investment banks were mostly mainly centered on creating and selling securities (e.g., debt and equity) to support businesses, governments, and large institutions to achieve their financing goals. Retail, private, corporate, business, and investment banks were traditionally separate entities. All can operate globally. In many cases, these different institutions have recently merged or acquired from another institution to create global financial powerhouses that now have all kinds of banks under one giant, global corporate umbrella.

The merger of all these types of banking firms has generated global economic challenges. For example, in the United States, the Glass-Steagall Act barred these two types-retail and investment banks-from being under the same corporate umbrella. The Glass-Steagall Act, enacted in 1932 during the Great Depression, officially called the 1933 Banking Reform Act, created the Federal Deposit Insurance Corporations

(FDIC) and implemented bank reforms, starting in 1932 and continuing through 1933. Those reforms are credited with providing the banking industry with stability and reduced risk for decades. It barred bank holding firms from buying certain financial businesses, among other items. This served to ensure that investment companies and banks stayed separate – until Glass-Steagall was repealed in 1999. Some analysts have criticized Glass-Steagall's repeal as one of the reasons for the financial crisis of 2007–8.

Due to the scale, breadth, and influence of US financial firms, this historic comparison point is essential to understand the effect of US firms on global firms. In 1999, once bank holding firms were able to own other financial services firms, the trend towards the creation of global financial powerhouses increased, blurring the line between which services were performed for the benefit of the financial firm itself, on behalf of the clients and which business was managed. International companies were also part of this trend, as they sought to serve their global financial interests alongside the most prominent and influential financial players in multiple markets. If a company has operations in twenty nations, for a more cost-effective and low-risk solution, it chooses two or three substantial, global banking ties. For example, one large bank can deliver services cheaper and better manage the exposure of the company's currency across multiple markets. One wide financial company will provide more sophisticated options and items for risk management. In certain situations, the problem has been that the team, on the other hand, of the multinational business transaction has turned out to be the global financial powerhouse itself, creating a conflict of interest that many would not feel would exist had Glass-Steagall not been repealed. The topic remains a subject of ongoing discussion around the world between businesses, financial firms, and policymakers. Meanwhile, the expanded services and capabilities of the significant financial powerhouses have significantly benefited from global businesses.

For example, Citigroup, based in the US, is the world's largest network of financial services, with 16,000 offices in 160 countries and territories, holding 200 million customer accounts. It is an economic powerhouse of retail, private, business, and investment banking operations, as well as asset management. The global reach of Citibank makes it a good banking partner for large global companies who want to be able to manage the financial needs of their employees and the operations of the company all around the world.

CHAPTER FIVE

THE GREAT DEPRESSION OF 1929

According to History.com, the Great Depression was the worst economic downturn in industrialized world history, which lasted from 1929 to 1939. It began after the October 1929 stock market crash that sent Wall Street into a panic and wiped out millions of investors. Consumer spending and investment decreased over the next several years, causing steep declines in industrial output and employment as failed firms laid-off workers. As the Great Depression hit its lowest point by 1933, about 15 million Americans were unemployed, and almost half of the country 's banks had failed.

CAUSES OF THE GREAT DEPRESSION

The U.S. economy rapidly expanded throughout the 1920s, and between 1920 and 1929, the nation's total wealth more than doubled, a period dubbed 'the Roaring Twenties.'

The stock market was the scene of reckless speculation, centered on New York's Wall Street stock exchange in New York City, where everyone, from millionaire tycoons to cooks and janitors, poured their savings into stocks. As a result, the stock price grew dramatically, peaking in August 1929.

By that time, production had already fallen, and unemployment had risen, leaving stock prices much higher than their actual value. Additionally, at that time, wages were low, consumer debt proliferated, the economy's agricultural sector was struggling because of drought and falling food prices, and banks had an excess of large loans that could not be liquidated.

During the summer of 1929, the American economy entered a mild recession as consumer spending slowed, and unsold goods started to pile up, which in turn slowed production. Nonetheless, stock prices began to increase, hitting stratospheric heights by the fall of the year, which could not be explained by expected future earnings.

Stock Market Crash of 1929

When panicked investors began selling overpriced securities on October 24, 1929 in masses, the stock-market collapse that some predicted ended up occurring. They traded a record 12.9 million shares that day, dubbed "Black Thursday."

Five days later, on October 29th, around 16 million shares

were listed, or "Black Tuesday," after another wave of panic struck Wall Street. Millions of securities ended up useless, and some creditors who purchased stocks "on the edge" (with borrowed money) were washed out thoroughly.

As consumer confidence disappeared in the aftermath of the stock market crash, the decline in spending and investment led factories and other companies to slow down production and start firing their employees. Wages fell and buying power decreased for those who were lucky enough to remain in jobs.

Many Americans compelled to purchase on credit plunged into debt, and the rate of foreclosures and repossessions gradually grew.

The Hoover Administration and Bank Runs

Despite assurances from President Herbert Hoover and other leaders that the crisis would run its course, over the next three years, matters continued to get worse. By 1930, 4 million Americans who were looking for work could not find any; and the amount rose to 6 million in 1931.

Meanwhile, the country's industrial production had shrunk by half. Bread lines, soup kitchens, and increasing numbers of homeless people became more and more common in cities across America. Farmers couldn't afford to harvest their crops, and they were forced into the fields to let them rot while people were starving elsewhere. In 1930 severe droughts in the Southern Plains brought high winds and dust from Texas to Nebraska, killing people, cattle, and crops. The "Dust Bowl" inspired a mass migration of people from the farmland to the cities in search of work.

The first of four waves of banking panics began in the fall of 1930, as large numbers of investors lost confidence in their banks' solvency and demanded cash deposits, forcing banks to liquidate loans to supplement their insufficient on-call cash reserves.

Bank runs swept the U.S. again in the spring and fall of 1931 and fall of 1932, and by the beginning of 1933, thousands of banks had closed.

In the face of this dire situation, Hoover 's administration tried to support failed banks and other institutions with government loans; the idea was that the banks would, in turn, lend to businesses, which would be able to hire their employees back.

Roosevelt Elected

Hoover, a Republican who had previously served as U.S. Secretary of Commerce, believed that government should not intervene directly in the economy, and was not responsible for creating jobs or providing economic relief for its citizens.

However, in 1932, with the country mired in the depths of the Great Depression and some 15 million unemployed (more than 20% of the U.S. population at the time), Democrat Franklin D. Roosevelt won an overwhelming presidential election victory.

By Inauguration Day (March 4, 1933), each U.S. state had ordered the closure of all remaining banks at the end of the fourth wave of banking panics in the United States. The Treasury also did not provide enough cash to compensate all government employees. Nevertheless, the FDR (as he was known) projected a calm energy and optimism, famously declaring "the only thing we need to fear is fear itself."

Roosevelt immediately took action to address the nation's economic woes, first announcing a four-day "bank holiday" during which all banks would close in order for Congress to enact reform legislation and reopen certain banks that were determined to be sound. In a series of talks, Roosevelt also began addressing the people directly on the radio, and these so-called "fireside chats" went a long way to restoring the pub.

His administration passed legislation during Roosevelt's first 100 days in office that sought to boost manufacturing and agricultural productivity, job generation and recovery stimulus.

In addition, Roosevelt sought to reform the financial system by creating the Federal Deposit Insurance Corporation (FDIC) to protect depositors' accounts, and the Securities and Exchange Commission (SEC) to regulate the stock market and prevent the kind of abuse that led to the 1929 crash.

The New Deal: A Road to Recovery

The Tennessee Valley Authority (TVA), which built dams and hydroelectric plants to regulate floods and provide power to the impoverished Tennessee Valley area, and the Works Progress Administration (WPA), a permanent jobs program which employed 8.5 million people from 1935 to 1943, were among the New Deal programs and agencies that helped the economy to recover from the Great Depression

By the time the Great Depression started, the US was the

only industrialized country in the world without some form of jobless insurance or social security. In 1935, Congress passed the Social Security Act, which provided the Americans with unemployment, disability, and old-age pensions for the first time.

After exhibiting early signs of recovery beginning in the spring of 1933, the economy started to grow over the next three years, over which actual (adjusted for inflation) GDP rose at an annual average rate of 9%.

A sharp recession hit in 1937, caused in part by the decision of the Federal Reserve to increase its reserve money requirements. Although the economy began to improve again in 1938, this second severe contraction reversed many of the production and employment gains and prolonged the effects of the Great Depression through the end of the decade.

Depression-era hardships also fueled the rise of extremist political forces in numerous European nations, most notably that of Adolf Hitler's Nazi regime in Germany. German aggression led to war breaking out in Europe in 1939, so the WPA turned its focus to strengthening the United States' defense resources, thus maintaining its neutrality.

African Americans in the Great Depression

One-fifth of the Americans who received federal relief during the Great Depression were African Americans, mostly in the rural south. But the Social Security Act of 1935 did not include farm and domestic work, two major sectors in which African Americans were employed, meaning that there was no safety net in times of uncertainty. Private employers could actually pay less without legal consequences, rather than fire domestic aid. And those relief programs that African Americans were eligible for on paper were rife in practice with discrimination since all relief programs were administered locally.

Women in the Great Depression

There was one group of Americans during the Great Depression who actually gained jobs: women. Between 1930 and 1940, the number of women employed in the United States increased 24% from 10.5 million to 13 million. Even though they had been steadily entering the workforce for decades, the financial pressures of the Great Depression led women to seek more and more jobs as male breadwinners lost their jobs. The decline in marriage rates of 22% between 1929 and 1939 also created an increase in the number of single women searching for employment.

Women had a powerful advocate in First Lady Eleanor Roosevelt during the Great Depression, who pushed her husband for more women in office — like Labor Secretary Frances Perkins, the first woman ever to occupy a cabinet position.

During the banking crisis, jobs available to women paid less but were more stable: nursing, teaching, and housework. They were replaced by a rise in secretarial positions in the fast-growing FDR government. But there was a catch: over 25% of the wage codes of the National Recovery Administration set lower wages for women, and jobs created under the WPA confined women to fields such as sewing and nursing that paid less than men's reserved roles.

Married women faced an additional hurdle: By 1940, 26 states had placed restrictions on their employment, known as marriage bars, because working wives were thought to be taking jobs away from older people – even if, in practice, men were occupying jobs that they did not like to do for even less pay.

End of Great Depression and Beginning of World War II

With Roosevelt's move to support Britain and France in the war against Germany and the other Axis Forces, the defense industry was geared up, generating more and more jobs for the private sector.

The Japanese attack on Pearl Harbor in December 1941 led to America's entry into World War II, and the factories of the nation reverted to the full mode of production.

This expanding industrial production, as well as widespread conscription starting in 1942, reduced the rate of unemployment below its level of pre-depression. The Great Depression had finally ended, and the U.S. turned its attention to the World War II global conflict.

GREAT DEPRESSION EFFECTS

According to Kimberly Amadeo, "the 1929 Great Depression devastated the US economy. A third of all banks failed. Unemployment rose to 25%, and homelessness increased. Housing prices plummeted 67%, international trade collapsed by 65%, and deflation soared above 10%. It took 25 years for the stock market to recover." (Kimberly 2020).

Overall, the Great Depression impacted nine main areas

tremendously.

Economy

The economy shrank by 50% within the first five years of the depression. In 1929 economic output as measured by gross domestic product was $105 billion. That is equivalent today to more than $1 trillion.

The economy had begun to decline in August 1929. By the year's end, 650 banks failed. According to the Economic Analysis Bureau, the economy shrank another 8.5% in 1930. In 1931 GDP dropped by 16.1% and in 1932 by 23.2%. By 1933 the world had suffered an economic contraction of at least four years. It produced only $56.4 billion, half of what it produced back in 1929.

Part of the contraction had been caused by deflation. According to the Bureau of Labor Statistics, the Consumer Price Index fell 27% between November 1929 and March 1933. Falling prices forced several businesses into bankruptcy.

New Deal spending boosted growth in GDP in 1934 by 17%. In 1935, it rose by another 11.1%, in 1936 by 14.3% and in 1937 by 9.7%.

Unfortunately, in 1938, the Government cut spending on New Deal. Depression came back, and the economy shrank by 6.3%.

World War II preparations sent growth to 7% in 1939 and 10% in 1940. Japan bombed Pearl Harbor the following year, and the United States went into World War II.

The New Deal and World War II spending shifted the economy from a pure, free market to a mixed economy. For its success, it depended far more on government spending. The Great Depression timeline shows this was a gradual, albeit necessary process.

Politics

The Depression impacted politics by shaking trust in unfettered capitalism. That type of economic laissez-faire was advocated by President Herbert Hoover, and it had failed.

People voted for Franklin Roosevelt as a result. His Keynesian economics promised to end the Depression with government spending. The economy after the New Deal grew by 17% in 1934, and unemployment dropped.

But FDR remained concerned about adding US $5 trillion in debt in today's dollar value to the national debt. In 1938, he slashed government expenditures and the crisis revived itself. Nobody wants to make that mistake any more. Instead, politicians rely on deficit spending, tax cuts, and other forms of expansive fiscal policy. That's created a US debt which is dangerously high.

The Depression ended in 1939 when government spending ramped up for World War II, contributing to the false assumption that military expenditure is beneficial for the economy. But it doesn't even rank among the four best ways to create jobs in the real world.

Social

Drought from the Dust Bowl destroyed crops in the Midwest. It lasted around ten years — too long to stay on for most farmers. To make matters worse, agricultural product prices have fallen to their lowest level since the Civil War. They became homeless as farmers left to look for work. In the 1930s, nearly six thousand shantytowns, called Hoovervilles, sprang up.

Prohibition was repealed in 1933. That enabled the government to impose taxes on now-legal alcohol sales. The FDR used the money to help make the New Deal pay.

The depression was so severe and lasting so long that many people felt the American Dream was dead. Instead, the vision shifted to provide a claim to material advantages. The American Dream that the founding fathers envisioned guaranteed the right to pursue one's own dream of happiness.

Unemployment

Unemployment reached 4.2% in 1928, the final year of the Roaring Twenties. That's below the natural unemployment rate. By 1930, it had more than doubled to 8.7%. By 1932, it had risen to 23.6%. It peaked in 1933, reaching approximately 25%. Nearly 15 million people are out of work. That's America's highest rate of unemployment ever recorded.

New Deal programs helped to reduce unemployment in 1934 to 21.7%, in 1935 to 20.1%, in 1936 to 16.9%, and in 1937 to 14.3%. By 1938, however, less vigorous government spending returned unemployment to 19%. Until 1941, it remained above 10%, according to an annual review of the unemployment rate.

Banking

A third of the nation's banks had failed during the Depression. Four thousand banks had failed by 1933. Depositors lost $140bn as a result.

People were amazed that banks used their deposits to invest in the stock market. They hurried to take out their money until it was too late. Even good banks were forced out of business by these "runs."

Stock Market

Between 1929 and 1932, the stock market lost 90% of its value. It didn't convalesce for 25 years. People lost their confidence in the markets in Wall Street. It wiped out businesses, banks, and individual investors.

Trade

As economies of countries worsened, trade barriers were erected to defend the local factories. Congress passed Smoot-Hawley tariffs in 1930, hoping to protect U.S. jobs.

It retaliated against other countries. That created trade blocs focused on national alliances and the currencies of trade. World trade, as measured in dollars, plummeted 66% and 25% in the total number of units. By 1939 it was still below its 1929 level.

Here's what happened to U.S. GDP during the first five years of the Depression: 1929: 103.6 billion dollars, 1930: 91.2 billion dollars, 1931: 76.5 billion dollars, 1932: 58.7 billion dollars, 1933: 56.4 billion.

Deflation

Between 1930 and 1932, prices fell by 30%. Deflation helped consumers whose income had dropped. This hurt farmers, businesses, and homeowners. Their mortgage payments slipped by 30%. As a result, many defaulted. They lost it all and became migrants looking for work wherever they could find it.

Long-Term Impact

The New Deal's success created expectations among Americans that the government would save them from any economic crisis. People also relied on themselves and each other to get through the Great Depression.

The FDR changed the gold standard to protect the interest of the dollar. That precedent was put to a complete end in 1973 by President Richard Nixon.

Many of today's landmarks were built under the New Deal public works programs. Iconic buildings include the Chrysler building in Dallas, the Rockefeller Center, and the Dealey Plaza. Bridges include the Golden Gate Bridge in San Francisco, the Triborough Bridge in New York, and the Overseas Highway in Florida Keys. Other public works during the Recession era include La Guardia Airport, Lincoln Tunnel, and Hoover Dam. They also built three entire towns: Greendale, Wisconsin; Greenhills, Ohio; and Greenbelt, Maryland.

CHAPTER SIX

THE REMOVAL OF GOLD STANDARD IN THE 1970s

"Throughout history, gold has been used as the currency of choice. The known earliest use was 600 B.C. in Lydia, which is Turkey today" (Kimberly 2020).

Gold was part of a naturally occurring compound known as electrum, used to make coins by the Lydians. By 560 B.C., the Lydians had discovered how to isolate the gold from the silver, producing the first genuinely gold coin. Croesus was the first king to use gold for coins, and his name lives on in the phrase "rich as Croesus."

The value of the coin in those days was based solely on the value of the metal, and the country with the most gold had the highest earners. As a result, Columbus and other settlers were sent into the New World by Spain, Portugal, and England. They needed more gold to be able to be wealthier than each other.

When gold was found at Sutter's Mill in 1848, the following year, it inspired the California Gold Rush, which helped unify Western America. It resulted in inflation at the time, and since 1834 the United States had already been on a de facto gold standard, and the influx of new gold led to rising prices.

The first U.S. paper currency was printed in 1861, by Treasury Secretary Salmon Chase. The 1900 Gold Standard Act established that gold was the only metal used to redeem paper currency. It set the gold value at $20.67 an ounce.

Throughout the booming world trade market, European countries wanted to standardize trades, and they embraced the gold standard by the 1870s. This guaranteed that the government would redeem every sum of paper money for its gold value, which implied that purchases would no longer have to be done by large gold bullion or coins because paper cash was therefore guaranteed to be valued at the real.

This colossal change also raised the trust required for successful global trade, and it came with its own risks: gold prices and currency rates dropped each time miners found major new gold deposits.

Congress created the Federal Reserve in 1913 to stabilize US gold and currency values. U.S. and European countries suspended the gold standard after World War I broke out so that they could print enough money to pay for their military involvement.

After the war, countries realized that they didn't have to bind their currency to gold and that doing so would actually harm the global economy. Countries, including the United States in 1919, quickly returned to a modified gold standard after the War. But the gold exchange standard triggered deflation and unemployment ran rampant in the world economy, and so by the 1930s, as the Great Depression hit its peak, countries began to relinquish the gold standard en masse. Finally, in 1933, the United States abandoned the gold standard entirely.

The Gold vs. Great Depression

The Great Depression hit the gold standard with full force, with countries being left with no choice but to abandon it. In 1929, as the stock market crashed, investors started to trade in currencies and commodities. When the gold price rose, people exchanged their dollars for gold. It worsened when banks began to collapse when people started hoarding gold because they didn't trust any financial institution.

In an attempt to make dollars more valuable and dissuade people from further depleting US gold reserves, the Federal Reserve kept raising interest rates, but it made the cost of doing business more expensive. Many companies went bankrupt, causing high unemployment rates.

The recently elected President at the time, Franklin D. Roosevelt, closed the banks on 6 March 1933 in reaction to a run on the gold reserves at New York's Federal Reserve Bank. By the time banks re-opened on March 13, they had switched to the Federal Reserve with all their money. They couldn't exchange dollars for gold anymore, and nobody could export gold.

On April 20 of 1933, the FDR ordered Americans to turn in their gold in exchange for dollars. This produced Fort Knox gold reserves. The USA soon held the most abundant supply of gold in the world.

The Gold Reserve Act banned private ownership of gold on January 30, 1934, except under license. It allowed the government to pay its debts in dollars, not gold, and authorized FDR to raise the gold price from $20.67 per ounce to $35 per ounce (which devalued the dollar accordingly).

HOW THE GOLD STANDARD ROSE

The gold standard is a monetary system where free convertibility of paper money into a fixed amount of gold is accomplished. In other terms, gold protects the value of money in such a monetary system. The development and formalization of the gold standard began between 1696 and 1812, as the introduction of paper money posed some problems.

The Constitution of the United States in 1789 granted Congress the sole right to coin money and the power to regulate its value. The creation of a united national currency enabled the standardization of a monetary system consisting, until then, of circulating foreign currency, mostly silver.

A bimetallic standard was adopted in 1792, with silver being in greater abundance as compared to gold at the time. While the officially adopted 15:1 silver-to-gold parity ratio properly mirrored the price ratio at the time, the value of silver declined steadily after 1793, driving gold out of circulation, according to Gresham's regulations.

Hard-money enthusiasts advocated a ratio that would bring gold coins back into circulation, not necessarily to push out silver, but to push out small-denomination paper notes issued by the then-hated US banks. A ratio of 16:1 was established that blatantly overvalued gold and reversed the situation, putting the US on a de facto gold standard.

By 1821, England became officially the first country to adopt a gold standard. The dramatic increase of global trade and production in the century brought large gold discoveries, which helped the gold standard to remain intact well into the next century. With all trade imbalances settled with gold between nations, governments had a strong incentive to stockpile gold for more difficult times. Today, those stockpiles still exist.

The international gold standard came into use in 1871 after Germany had embraced it. By 1900, most developed nations had been tied to the gold standard. Ironically, the United States was one of the last states to join. In fact, throughout the 19th century, a strong silver lobby prevented gold from being the sole monetary standard within the US.

The gold standard was at its peak from 1871 through 1914. There had been virtually ideal political conditions in the world during this time. Governments worked very well together to make the system work, but with the outbreak of the Great War in 1914, all this changed forever.

PROTOCOLS OF MONEY

THE FALL AND REMOVAL OF THE GOLD STANDARD

Political alliances changed with World War I, international indebtedness rose, and government finances declined. While the gold standard was not suspended after the war, it was in limbo, demonstrating its failure to hold in both good and bad times. This created a lack of confidence in the gold standard and only exacerbated economic problems. It became increasingly clear that the world wanted something more flexible to build the global economy on.

At the same time, a desire among nations to return to the idyllic years of the gold standard remained strong. As the supply of gold continued to fall behind the global economy's growth, the British pound sterling and the US dollar became the reserve currencies worldwide. Smaller countries started to hold more of these currencies, rather than gold. The result was an accentuated gold consolidation into the pockets of a few great nations.

The 1929 stock market crash was just one of the difficulties of the post-World War I world. The pound and the French franc were horribly misaligned with other currencies; Germany was still stifled by war debts and repatriations; commodity prices crumbled, and banks were overextended. Many countries sought to protect their gold stock by raising interest rates to encourage investors to keep their deposits intact, rather than converting them into gold. These higher interest rates only worsened issues for the global economy. In 1931, England's gold standard was suspended, leaving vast gold reserves only for the US and France.

Then, in 1934, the U.S. government revalued gold from

$20.67/oz to $35/oz, raising the amount of paper money it cost to purchase one ounce to boost the economy further. Since other nations could convert their current gold reserves into more U.S. dollars, there was instantly a drastic devaluation of the currency. This higher gold price increased the exchange of gold into U.S. dollars, enabling the U.S. to corner the gold market in effect. Gold production soared, so there was enough in the world by 1939 to replace all of the global circulatory currency.

As World War II came to an end, the leading Western powers met to develop the Bretton Woods Agreement, which until 1971 would shape the basis for global currency markets. All national currencies were priced within the Bretton Woods system in relation to the U.S. dollar and were the dominant reserve currency. In turn, the dollar was convertible to gold at a set cost of $35 per ounce. While more indirectly, the global financial system continued to operate on a gold standard.

Over time, the deal has led to a new relationship between the gold and the US dollar. A decreasing dollar generally means rising prices for gold over the long term. This isn't always true in the short term, and the relationship can be tenuous at best. However, the correlation is still biased towards the reverse (negative on the correlation study), so gold typically declines as the dollar rises.

The U.S. had 75% of the world's monetary gold at the end of WWII, and the dollar was the only currency that was still directly backed by gold. However, when the world rebuilt itself after WWII, the US saw its gold reserves fall steadily when money flowed to war-torn nations and its strong import demand.

Senator John F. Kennedy issued a statement at the late stages of his presidential campaign that, if chosen, he would not seek to devalue the currency, with a surplus transforming to deficit in 1959 and increasing concerns of foreign nations starting to reclaim their dollar-denominated gold reserves.

A Gold Pool, which included the US and a number of European nations, stopped selling gold on the London market in 1968, facilitating the market to freely determine the gold price. The Gold Pool collapsed when member nations were unable to cooperate fully in maintaining the retail interest at the US gold price. Belgium and the Netherlands both cashed in dollars for gold in the following years, with Germany and France expressing similar intentions. From 1968 until 1971, only central banks were able to trade $35/oz with the U.S. By making available a pool of gold reserves, the market price for gold could be kept in line with the official rate of parity. This eased the pressure on member nations to value their currencies to sustain their strategies for export-led growth. And foreign nations' increasing competitiveness, combined with debt monetization to pay for social programs and the Vietnam War, quickly started to weigh on America's balance of payments. Late 1960s high inflationary environment sucked the last bit of air out of the gold standard.

In August 1971, Britain requested payment in gold, forcing a hand from Nixon and officially closing the gold doors. It was official by 1976; gold would no longer define the dollar, thus marking the end of any gold standard semblance.

Nixon severed the full convertibility of U.S. dollars to gold in August 1971. The international currency market, which had become increasingly dependent on the dollar since the enactment of the Bretton Woods Agreement, lost its formal link to gold with this decision. The US dollar joined the age of fiat money, and by extension, the global financial system that it has sustained effectively.

GOLD STANDARD ADVANTAGE

The benefit of a gold standard is that the value of the money is supported by a fixed asset. Gold standard proponents say it provides the economy with a self-regulating and stabilizing effect. The Government will only print as much currency as the nation has in gold under the gold standard. This discourages inflation, something which happens when so much capital is chasing too little goods. It also discourages government deficits and debt that can't exceed the gold supply.

The more productive nations are rewarded with a gold standard. For example, when they export, they get gold. They can print more money out with more gold in their reserves. That is enhancing investment in their profitable export businesses.

Exploration spurred the gold standard. It is why the New World was discovered in the 1500s by Spain and other European countries. To improve their wealth, they had to acquire more gold. It also spurred the California and Alaska Gold Rush during the 1800s.

GOLD STANDARD DISADVANTAGE

One issue with a gold standard is that the size and health of a country's economy became dependent on its gold supply. The economy is not reliant on the creativity of its people and businesses. Countries with no gold at all have a competitive disadvantage.

The US never experienced the problem. After Australia, it was the second-largest gold mining country in the world. Gold mining in the US occurred in 12 western states on federally owned lands. Nevada was the primary source, according to the National Mining Association. Many developing countries were significant producers of gold, too.

The gold standard makes countries obsessed with gold-keeping. They are missing the more significant task of improving the business climate. The Federal Reserve had raised interest rates during the Great Depression. It wanted to make dollars worthier and prevent people from demanding gold, but to stimulate the economy, it should have been lowering rates.

Government actions to protect its gold reserves have caused significant economic fluctuations. Also, the U.S. economy suffered five major recessions for this reason between 1890 and 1905. These facts were mentioned by Edward M. Gramlich in his remarks at the Eastern Economic Association's 24th annual conference on 27 February 1998. Gramlich was a member of the Federal Reserve Board of Governors.

CHAPTER SEVEN

INTRODUCTION TO
FRACTIONAL RESERVE BANKING

Meaning of Fractional Reserve Banking

Fractional reserve banking is a system in which only a fraction of bank deposits are backed up and available for withdrawal by actual cash on hand. This is done to expand the economy theoretically by freeing out lending capital.

Generally, reserve implies some amount of money retained in the organization and not dispersed among the shareholders and other stakeholders. Bank reserves are made according to the same logic. Bank Reserve can also mean the deposits of funds that are not loaned to customers of the bank. The only variance is that bank reserves are always made in cash, whereas accounting reserves can also be made in regular business as provisions (e.g., obsolete stock provision), allowances (e.g., bad debt allowance), and accruals (e.g., accrued liabilities), which do not have cash equivalents but are made as double entries in an accounting system.

According to the Business Dictionary, banks can make primary reserves (to meet the needs of daily operations) and secondary reserves (to meet the requirements of emergency liquidity). Primary reserves are funds needed to finance regular bank transactions, uncollected checks, and comply with the provisions of legal/obligatory reserves. Primary reserves cannot be used (loaned out or invested), but they can be used in the event of a liquidity crisis when heavy money withdrawal begins by depositors.

Secondary reserves are defined by bank as investment funds in short-term marketable securities (e.g., treasury bills), which act as assistance to primary reserves, being a supplementary source of liquidity.

The fractional reserve forms part of primary reserves of banks. It is a financial sector in which cash-on-hand supports only a fraction of bank deposits and is accessible for withdrawal.

Therefore, the fractional reserve ensures some percentage (fraction) of each money paid, which is required by a bank to be kept on hand and cannot be loaned to anybody. The central bank sets the size of the percentage.

THE ORIGINS OF FRACTIONAL BANKING RESERVE

"A "bank" is a corporation that raises funds both by taking in "deposits" (or generating account balances) and issuing loans from the accumulated funds. A moneylender who draws on his own wealth alone is not a banker" (Federal 2012). In ordinary modern usage, "Deposit" implies a debt claim, an IOU provided by the banker and kept by the "depositor," which the banker is obligated to return in compliance with the conditions of the contract. We may distinguish from a "time investment" that the banker is obligated to reimburse in the future only at a specified date, and a "demand deposit," which gives the customer the legal right to "on-demand" repayment, that is, whenever the customer chooses (the bank is open on any day).

Deposit-taking has historically grown out of the coin-changing and safekeeping business. Italian medieval money-changers would swap coins from one town (for a fee) to those from another. Some traveling merchants, who brought in one type of coins, would, for the time being, choose to hold "on account" balances, preferring to receive coins of another type later when it was more convenient. Goldsmiths, artisans who made gold jewelry, and candlesticks, were the earliest deposit-takers in London, and they were also coin-changers. They had safe-keeping in the vaults, like the Italian coin-changers, where they stored their own silver and gold.

A key to fractional-reserve banking development was that vault-keepers (money-changers and goldsmiths) started offering payment services through deposit transfer. The earliest record of deposit transfer payment emanates in Italy around

1200 AD. Before deposits became transferable, suppose Alphonso wanted to pay Bartolomeo (say) 100 ounces of coined silver, both of which were customers of the same vault keeper. Al would go to the vault-keeper, have him weigh the necessary amount of coins, and carry the coins back to Bart, who would then have to bring the coins back to the vault-keeper to get them weighed up again and put them back in the vault. There was a considerable inconvenience, not to say risk, in transporting the coins across the town and back. And weighing the coins had fees to pay. At the end of the day, Al's cash balance or charge on the vault-keeper will go down by 100 ounces (plus transaction fees), and Bart's will go up by 100 ounces (minus transaction fees).

A less complicated and safer way to make such payment for Al and Bart is to meet at the bank, and simply tell the banker to transfer 100 ounces on his books by writing down Al's account balance and writing up's Bart's balance. There's no need to measure or move coins, or even handle them at all. Payment was now made not through the handing over of coins but through handing over of claims to coins.

Other methods for authorizing the transfer of deposits were often more convenient, and the three-party meeting in the banker's office soon displaced. For instance, Al could perhaps sign a written authorization, which we now call check. We have electronic transfer of funds today, but all these methods accomplish the same aim, which is to allow a move of funds from one account to another.

Several of the earliest deposit-taking was easy warehousing, in which the deposited coins were simply stored, and the actual same coins would be given back to the depositor on request, assuming all store fees had been paid out. (Such a claim on the warehouse is, in legal terms, a "settlement" and not a debt.) In the early Middle Ages, a customer who wanted this type of storage would bring the coins in a sealed bag into the vault. The warehouseman would not open the bag. For a particular bag of coins that Al or Bart might say, such a specific bag of coins was still in the vault. If the contents of the bags were recorded in the books (which they didn't need to have been), we could say that there was indeed an ounce of coined silver in the vault for every ounce of coined silver stated by depositors. This arrangement, which reflects today's business of renting safety deposit boxes, is often defined as "100% reserve banking," but it is not banking at all, strictly speaking, but simply warehousing.

As payment by deposit transfer became popular, goldsmiths and coin-changers noticed that customers who did not mainly want storage but economic payment facilities, could be given a specific kind of deal. The vault-keeper is a lender in a "fractional reserve" contract, being able to lend out any of the deposited funds. A client who wanted that kind of account would carry loose coins to the bank in the early Middle Ages. The coins could be mixed with the coins of other depositors, whereas there is no vital explanation for mixing in the money warehousing. The customer would receive a redeemable claim entitling him to retrieve on demand equivalent coins but not to recover the identical coins he brought in. Now, the account is a debt claim and not a bail. All the coins in the vault are a fraction of the deposits which are directly in demand. We can describe them as a reserve to fulfill the claims of redemption that are actually to be made.

Later, perhaps starting in the 1400s, banks issued new deposit receipts that could be signed over, making them today something like traveler's checks. They soon provided them in bearer form (no signing-over needed) and round denominations for the convenience of their customers. Banknotes, typically on demand, paper currency claims on banks that were payable to the bearer (whoever put them in), as a currency, they can be transferred anonymously, and without bank involvement (unlike transfers of deposits that need to be recorded on books). In the mid-1600s, London goldsmiths issued banknotes. Banks also held fractional reserves against their total liabilities to the banknotes.

EXPLANATION OF THE FRACTIONAL RESERVE SYSTEM

Everybody knows just what the money is. We use the money in our everyday lives. For us, money means banknotes in our bank accounts and cash in hand. Economists define money as an equivalent that is used in today's world as a measure of the goods. In other words, money is a universal means of exchange, understandable to all.

Do we know where money comes from? I think most of us would be responding actively. We can earn money, we can inherit money, we can gain lottery money, we can get money as a birthday present, and we can borrow money from a bank for sure. Thus, it is pretty clear to a physical person where money comes from.

And what about the supply of State money, or where is the government receiving funds from? Textbooks will claim the currency is emitted by the Central Bank, and then this currency is put into the financial system. This currency may also be called "physical money" or "money outside." This is a deal. But Commercial banks also create money in the form of loans and credits. We cannot touch this money. This money is called "deposit money" or "deposit money" and is generated through the fractional reserve system. I took the names of 'outside money' and 'inside money' from the article on the fractional reserve banking published on the Federal Reserve Bank of Atlanta website because, in my opinion, they clearly reflect the significance of the subject (Federal Reserve Bank of Atlanta).

So how can a bank earn money? If a bank takes a deposit shortly, it will turn into a loan, which in turn will become another deposit, and so on. This is how "inside money" is created, via the deposit-lending process. But what role does it play here in the fractional reserve?

Central bank defines the amount of the fractional reserve. If the central bank wants commercial banks to create more or less "inside money," it can adjust the requirements of the fractional reserve to allow banks keep more or fewer reserves and therefore produce more or less "inside money". If the Central Bank sets lower reserve requirements, banks can lend more money, which in turn will become new deposits, which thus will be created by the fractional reserve system to create the amount of money. And vice versa: higher requirements for the fractional reserve will result in less money to lend out and less money supply.

This process of making money by deposit-lending and changing reserve requirements forms the basis for the concept of money multiplier, which I will describe in more detail. If we turn back to money supply and currency emission, we should mention the fact that banknotes and coins issued by the Central Bank should be backed up by any physical commodity, which is bank assets. But are any bank assets backed by the "inside money" – loans and credits? Do they even have anything to back them up? Can we talk about the Fiat money when it comes to the fractional reserve system? In short, fiat money means currency that has been issued by a government that is not backed by a physical commodity (Investopedia. Fiat money). But as we know, the fractional reserve is just a certain percentage of each deposited sum, which in turn means that the bank fund has been unable to back any given loan. So is the fractional reserve system encouraging the creation of fiat money, and what can be the consequences? Let's turn now to the theory and study the above-mentioned concepts and a few more to find answers to these and other questions.

THEORIES AND CONCEPTS

"Money supply concept is the starting point for understanding the role of the fractional reserve role within the financial system" (Valkonen 7).

Money supply

Money supply means the "the entire stock of currency and other liquid instruments in the economy of a country at a given time" (Investopedia. Money supply). Cash, coins, checks, and savings accounts are included in the money supply. In the money supply, different types of money are usually classified as M0, M1, M2, M3, M4, and MB. M0 includes making the rounds currency (banknotes and coins), and central bank reserves. M1 includes currency in circulation, current accounts (checking), and deposit accounts, which can be transferred through checks.

M2 includes circulation currency, saving accounts, and bank deposits bearing no interest. M3 includes M1, and other deposits and deposit certificates from non-government (or the private sector). There is also category M3C, which includes M3 plus foreign exchange deposits.

M4 includes M1 plus deposits from the private sector and investments in the capital market (which are highly liquid government or short-term corporate debt instruments traded in the money market: promissory notes, treasury bills, etc.). Some sources also assign M5 group, which includes M4 and Building-Society deposits (Building-Society is a form of financial entity that provides its members with financial services (Investopedia. Definition of Building Society). MB refers to money from the central bank. All the rest, Ms is money related to the commercial banks.

Banks can expand the money market by lending money that they don't really possess but are instead allowed to create, lend, and spend. Having, for example, 10% in reserve, a bank can lend around 90% of the funds that a bank does not hold (it simply means that a bank will lend 0.90 EUR out of every 1 EUR in each deposit). In other words, "the fractional reserve system enables banks to lend the amount they have in reserve many times over." (2010, O'Leary, 11). Banks create money by creating new debts, and no physical commodities back up this money. Depending on the form of loan, M2 and M3 money types increase with the usage of the fractional reserve system banks.

The Fed (US Central Bank) provides the following definition for the money supply: "a group of safe assets that households and businesses can use to make payments or hold as short-term investments" (Federal Reserve System Board of Governors 2014). Key term 'safe' here. But are these assets really safe, or do they appear safe? In fact, banks lend money that they don't own to people, who then spend or further invest the money they don't own. And in general, just a tiny percentage of these loans are really secured by cash from actual products. Now let's move on to the concept of money multiplications to understand the nature of the role of the fractional reserve in the deposit-lending chain.

Money multiplier

The multiplier effect of money falls in as commercial banks make money by lending to each other. By Investopedia, "the size of the effect of the multiplier depends on the percentage of deposits that banks will keep as reserves. In other words, money is used to create more money and is calculated by dividing total bank deposits by the requirement of the reserve.

If speaking in numbers, the picture looks like this: a person puts 100,000 EURO on the bank account, say. Imagine that a bank has a reserve requirement of 10%. Thus 10,000 EURO will be held in cash as a backup from the initial deposit. All remaining amount – EUR 90 000 – a bank can lend out. Indeed, a bank took 100 000 EURO (actual cash) and turned it into EUR 190 000 by lending out 90 000 EURO. Can a bank grow its initial deposit steadily? Yes, it could.

There is also a very skeptical opinion about the multiplier effect of money, expressed by Forbes' economics editor John Tamny. He says that money multiplier in that sense is a myth that without people, there would be no money multiplier effect. In other words, without buyers, there are no salesmen, and without demand, there is no supply. Banks could not lend deposited money if there were no borrowers, and the initial deposit of EUR 100 000 will never multiply into EUR 1 000 000 in real life without changing hands adequate times. If no one makes deposits, bank will never have money to lend out. Some skeptics blame the fractional reserve mechanism and multiplier impact for causing capital to be created "from thin air," which is a kind of moral hazard (Tamny 2012). Tamny says banks are actually doing their job: they are lending money that one person puts in their care to another, who wants to borrow, and there's nothing "immoral" about it.

Banks, of course, could operate on a reserve requirement of 100%, but in this case, they would no longer be banks, but "warehouses for money," which would charge depositors a premium for the right to deposit their money (Tamny 2012). This system will not allow the money to "work," the saved money value will decline every day, which will eventually lead to devaluation of the currency of the state. The fractional reserve allows banks to pay compensation (percentage) by making loans to others who need credit here and now for the money that people don't need immediately and compensate for those expenses. According to Tamny, that is how the fractional reserve actually works.

To summarize all of the above, there are two views about

the multiplier effect of money: theoretical and practical. The first gives a pretty clear calculated example of how banks may grow money using the fractional reserve, while the second claims that the money multiplier will never operate without people who are making deposits and taking credits. Also, there is the opinion that a fractional reserve is a standard tool in terms of normal business management, nothing about making money "from thin air". Business is designed to make profits, and so do the banks.

FIAT MONEY

Fiat money generally means the currency, which is not supported by a physical commodity. What physical products does a bank have? It is cash for sure. A bank can increase the initial hypothetical deposit from EUR 100.00 to EUR 1 million, using 10% of the reserve requirement. The hypothetical bank only has EUR 100 000 in cash that is required by the fractional reserve system. All the remaining amount 900 000 EURO-is not backed by cash, as banks do not operate on a reserve requirement of 100%. So can we call fiat money for these EUR 900 000?

Paul O'Leary, American Doctor of Jurisprudence, real estate, and forensic appraiser, explains what fiat money is using the US dollar's example. O'Leary states that although the U.S. dollar banknote is issued in the U.S. and used as money, it is not a dollar, in fact, but a "substitute dollar" since it cannot be redeemed for any gold or silver (O'Leary 2010, 15). And that's how it works in the world: paper banknotes are not secured by assets, so they're called "fiat money." Such paper banknotes are issued by each country's national central banks (in the Eurozone, there is also the European Central Bank, which has the power to release and print euro banknotes).

What are the Banks doing? The fractional reserve system enables banks to lend out the amount of money they have in reserve several times over. Banks generate liquidity by giving credits (increase money supply), and those credits are not actually backed by actual cash. O'Leary states, "Money is created by the creation of new debt" (O'Leary 2010, 11), and no asset supports the debt. The trick is that only a small percentage of this created money is backed by actual cash (which is in reserve). In contrast, all the remaining money is created and destroyed continuously (money is created when a bank makes loans and destroyed when this loan is repaid).

So can one call this "created" money fiat money? Yes, it can. Will it have a positive or negative impact on the economy of the State? Well, that is a topic to think about. Actually, the banks don't print their own money, but by a continuous deposit-lending process, they increase money supply. The actual monetary base of banks is in its reserves. If we remember M-types, banks particularly increase M2 and M3 forms of capital (just to remember, M2 is circulation currency, saving accounts and bank deposits carrying no interest, and M3 is private-sector deposits). Deposits are considered to be less liquid than the monetary base (i.e., lending can deposit excess), and this is a potential risk of the situation when the demand or need for credits is higher than the supply of deposits. This situation is also known as "inflation on demand" If a bank is unable to meet the demand, short-term liquidity shortfalls can emerge.

In order to deal with liquidity shortfalls, banks must ask the last-resort lender for assistance. Lender of last resort is "an institution that offers loans to banks, usually the central bank of a country." Resort lenders are central banks operated by countries and are supposed to provide Banks with emergency liquidity assistance.

Here comes the question: does the fractional reserve system take into account the risks of the banks making loans? Certainly not. Surely, it can meet the one-time need for cash on hand, which occurs during a day, but it cannot help with more liquidity problems when a bank cannot meet the demand of depositors, and the bank falls below its reserve requirements, experiencing liquidity squeeze.

If 100% reserve requirement occurred, interest on deposits would not be accumulated, and no loans would be generated. Therefore, we can say that the primary purpose of the fractional reserve system is not to protect from risks but to enable banks to function naturally.

Gold Standard conspiracy theory

The fact that the primary goal of the fractional reserve scheme is not to protect from liquidity risks causes arguments over what this system's actual purpose is. Is it just a base for the activity of regular banks, or is it something else? From this point of view, the system of fractional reserves is the subject of followers of conspiracy theories.

There are several conspiracy theories, and they are about how world-renowned wealthy Jewish bankers like the Rothschild family control governments and the world. I decided to study the Gold Standard Theory, which explains where the roots grow from the banking system's point of view.

In his book "Conspiracy Theories in American History," Knight, P. says that "at the most basic level conspiracy theory blames the current, unwelcome state of affairs on a secret group's concerted conspiracy. It is, in effect, the interpretation of history that claims that things are not always what they seem and that things have not just tumbled out by coincidence in the usual, more-or-less random fashion, but they have only got that because someone with evil intentions planned it this way "(Knight 2003, 16).

There are many conspiracy theories, and the fractional reserve banking, in particular, is a part of the conspiracy theory of Gold Standard as an instrument for controlling money supply. The fractional reserve under this theory is an instrument for controlling the money supply.

The basis for conspiracy theories, according to Knight, lies in banking history. Gold was used as money in the past as it had a number of essential characteristics: it was easily divisible, it was portable, it had value itself, it was scarce (rare), and it was robust (Knight 2003, 285). But, in the age of growing capitalism in Europe and the US, the scarcity of gold became very unattractive as a characteristic of money when the economy demanded increasing financing, exchange, and easily circulated medium. By the year 1800, it became quite clear that the gold coin can no longer fulfill the demands of the growing capitalist system. The system demanded a significant rise in the money supply but was not able to be provided by either gold or silver. The Bank of England was the first bank to declare that there was wealth, not only in gold and silver. The Bank operated on a gold reserve and issued banknotes, which were exchangeable in gold and silver. Because these metals were scarce, it was quite clear that not enough metal was accessible to redeem every banknote at 100% (par) value. Subsequently, the idea of fractional reserve banking was based on statistical likelihood (and likelihood based on common sense) that only a fraction of banknote holders would ever redeem their gold or silver paper notes.

Conspiracy theorists suggest that through this action, the Bank of England deliberately cheated people by issuing banknotes that could not be redeemed in an emergency.

Scottish banks, at the same time, did not use any specific reserve ratios but allowed competition between banks to sort out "good" banks from "bad" ones. If "bad" banks failed, there was double blame for losses to their management. In contrast to the Bank of England with the gold-convertible money, some experts named the Scottish approach (it also had the name of "free banking"), with its competitive capital more stable and resilient (Knight 2003, 286).

US legislation bridges these two systems. States adopted a system of chartered banks, with authority to issue banknotes on paper, backed by precious metals, and these banknotes were always convertible. The banks could either "suspend" specie payments during panics, or fail to convert paper notes to gold or silver.

The bank, which was unable to convert paper money into specie, was losing its authority to do business, according to legislation. So there was healthy competition among banknotes, which let people know which banknotes were reliable enough.

Before the Civil War (i.e., before 1861), the US banking system was entirely tied to a gold standard: banks issued competitive gold-backed notes.

During the Civil War, the Union government of Abraham Lincoln needed additional revenue to finance the war, and it suspended all redemption of gold but authorized the printing of $450 million in paper notes (Knight 2003, 286). These notes are not immediately redeemable in gold, but at a future date, it has a "promise" to be redeemed. In addition, by placing a 10% tax on all non-national banknotes, the Union removed competition with government money issued by the national banks. Thus, the link to gold was temporarily destroyed, and competition in the issue of banknotes between banks ended.

The US suffered from national deflation after the Civil War. Simultaneously, there was the boom of new silver discoveries, and one silver ounce was traded for 17 gold ounces (Knight 2003, 287), and this gave investment ground. Domestic and foreign speculators poured silver into the treasury of the United States and took cash. The government and banker J.P. Morgan were very close to bankruptcy. Morgan gave a massive loan to the Government. It was a matter for conspiracy theorists to claim that by controlling the gold standard, bankers like Morgan, Carnegie, and Rockefeller manipulated the economy of the State.

In 1920, immediately after England, the US banking system went off the gold standard and began to act within international currency exchanges (Knight 2003, 288).

Thus, conspiracy theorists claim that the Rockefellers

control the supply of state money with the help of the Rothschilds from England and the Bank of England, and the FED, in a political context, is merely an instrument for this with the power to set the requirements for fractional reserves for national banks.

Fractional Reserve Advantages and Disadvantages

The benefit of keeping fractional reserves for the bank is evident: it earns interest on the lent-out funds. A few commentators say that Fractional Reserve Banking must be a fraud: the gain is all on the side of the bank, and no customer would agree if she realized what the bank was up to. But this claim assumes the bank's customers have no advantages. In fact, the customers of the bank have clear benefits, at least under competition. In order to compete for customers, banks offering fractional-reserve accounts charge zero storage fees and even pay interest on deposits, to the point where the interest they pay is short of the interest they only earn by enough to cover the operating costs of the bank for security and payment services. In this way, Fractional Reserve Banking creates a synergy between payment services (checkable deposits, banknotes) and intermediation (pooling funds from savers to lend to selected borrowers). As it is possible to lend out deposited funds that are not needed as reserves, depositors enjoy lower storage fees (or zero) and receive interest for their deposit balance.

Unlike money warehousing, fractional-reserve banking savings do carry a disadvantage in the form of increased default risk. If the bank's investments go sour, the depositor may not continue receiving interest. Alternatively, the warehouse will not make any savings. Historically, in sound banking systems, the risk of loss was a small fraction of one percent before deposit insurance, while the interest was more than one percent, and the sum of savings in interest and storage fees was even greater.

The economist George Selgin looked at the record of the London goldsmith bankers and debunked the myth that they pulled a fraudulent switcheroo at the beginning of Fractional Reserve Banking practice, promising 100% reserves but holding less. In the mid-1600s, Goldsmith bank accounts became enormously popular as they gave interest on demand deposits.

Fractional Reserve Banking provides a more economical means of providing payment services with payment by account transfer. A money warehouse or 100% reserve institution could also offer account transfer payments, but its services would be considerably more expensive. Without fractional reserves, the other bank payment instrument, redeemable banknotes circulating in round denominations, simply cannot exist. For a fractional-reserve bank, banknotes are feasible because the bank does not have to assess the storage fees to cover its costs. It can let the notes circulate anonymously and at face value, unburdened by fees, and cover their costs through interest income. An issuer with 100% reserve notes that circulate would need to assess somebody's storage costs, but would not be able to assess them on unknown noteholders. There are no known historical instances of 100% unencumbered reserve notes circulating by storage fees.

The introduction and public acceptance of fractionally backed demand deposits and banknotes, under a gold or silver standard, means that the economy needs less gold or silver in its vaults to supply the amount of money balances that the public wants to hold. Thus, income is provided at a lower resource cost that is, with less labor and capital devoted to extracting or importing precious metals and fashioning them into bars or coins. Looking at the change in balance sheets from money warehouses to fractional reserve banks, the economy can now fund productive commitments where it only held metal ahead of time. You may export gold and import productive machinery. Adam Smith lauded this development in Scotland as a driver of economic growth for his region.

FRACTIONAL RESERVE BANKING EFFECT ON THE PROCESS OF MONEY SUPPLY

With banks holding fractional Federal Reserve dollar reserves (notes and deposit claims on the Fed 's books, the sum of which is called "the monetary base"), when the Fed increases the amount of Federal Reserve dollars by $1 billion, the banking system generally creates multiple deposit dollars. The total stock of publicly held money ("M1") increases.

THE PROBLEMS OF BANK RUNS, CRISES, AND FINANCIAL INSTABILITY

Perhaps the leading argument in favor of government banking regulation is the argument that a fractional-reserve banking system is inherently fragile and thus needs insurance on reserves. The argument rests on three premises:

A fractional-reserve uninsured banking system is inherently prone to runs and (due to "contagion") panic. (A run means that many depositors seek to withdraw at the same time, for fear of a reduced payout if they wait. Panic means many banks suffer at the same time.)

- There are net harmful effects for runs and panics.
- Deposit insurance may reduce runs and panics below their laissez-faire level at a lower cost than it would benefit.

A run at fractionally backed bank deposits is always possible. In theory, even a run can be self-justifying against such deposits: if a run forces the bank to conduct a hasty sale of illiquid assets, the bank may receive such a reduced value for its assets that it becomes insolvent (liabilities exceed assets) so that all depositors can no longer be paid in full. Some economic theorists have jumped from that theoretical possibility to the conclusion that fractional-reserve banks are inherently run-prone in practice. (The best-known statement is an article by Douglas Diamond and Phillip Dybvig in 1983.) According to this view, a run can occur at any time, anywhere, on any bank, triggered by nothing more than random fears or events which have no basis in the solidity of the target bank.

But are these real-world deposit contracts fragile? Historical evidence shows no. Please consider: If real-world deposit contracts were really as vulnerable as the self-justifying-run theory assumes, it would be a mystery how they survived decades of Darwinian banking competition prior to the first government deposit insurance schemes. Would it not have come to rule the game in a more robust arrangement?

The theory of runs that suits the historical record best is that runs take place, not randomly, but when depositors get poor news suggesting that their bank might be (pre-run) already insolvent. Depositors run on receiving such news because if assets are already too small to pay all depositors back, the last in line gets little or nothing. Unlike the self-justifying-run hypothesis, the bad-news theory describes why runs usually took place during the start of recessions (when bad news came from bank lenders filing bankruptcy) and explains why countries that did not threaten their banks through regulatory sanctions (e.g., Scotland, Canada) very rarely witnessed runs and almost no panics.

What makes a contract to deposit run prone? Guess the depositors are rational. There needs to be a more substantial expected payoff to arrive earlier than later in order to redeem one's deposit. This implies that on-demand, the deposit is unconditionally redeemable (and that the bank pays on a first-come-first-served basis) and that the default is likely to be serviced on the last claim. It suffices to change one of these two criteria to make an account non-run-prone. Firstly, the contract for deposit can make redemption conditional rather than unconditional. An essential historical example was the 'notice of withdrawal clause' included in their deposit contracts by many savings banks and trust firms. If withdrawals were too large for a bank to satisfy without suffering severe losses as a result of hastily liquidating assets, the banker had the option of postponing redemption for 60 or 90 days by allowing notice of intent to redeem to be issued too far in advance.

More importantly, banks made default unlikely by providing credible assurances to their depositors that the bank will retain solvency, that is, assets sufficient to pay for the last in line in full, even under awful conditions. Before deposit insurance, banks kept far higher capital than they do today, in the 20% region, to provide credible assurance. They spent much more conservatively, and they had much less risk of large losses of assets. They avoided high default risk loans, a high risk of loss from interest-rate movements, and illiquid (hard to resell) loans. For example, banks that relied on demand deposits and banknotes did not make long-term fixed-rate housing loans. They traded mostly in short-term, high-quality, liquid business IOUs, which were then called "bills of exchange" and are now called "financial paper." In certain nations, banks had an additional backstop in the form of the right of their owners. To call for more capital if otherwise, depositors went unpaid. Shareholders had extended liability for the bank's debts and unlimited liability in some systems.

Of course, the historical record shows that runs and banking panics were a problem in the U.S. during the pre-Fed or "State Financial" era (1863 - 1913), and also under the watch of the Fed during the early years of the Great Depression. So, it is clear that run-proneness and panics are not inherent in the banking of fractional reserves. When we look at a pattern across nations, that is what we find: countries such as Canada, Scotland, Sweden, and Switzerland, where the financial networks had minimal restrictions on entry, note-issue, branching, and capitalization, had virtually no problem with runs and no problem with panics, as compared to the more restricted and thus weaker banking systems of the United States and Britain.

The federal and state ban on interstate branching made the U.S. banking system fragile, and even branching within many states. Branch banking limits reduced asset diversification and sources of deposits, indirectly limited capitalization, and hindered effective reserve allocation. Sparsely diversified and thinly capitalized banks were unable to provide reliable solvency assurances, making them more vulnerable to runs of "bad news."

The U.S. system was also made fragile by federal banknote issue restrictions that also prevented banks from meeting peak currency demands. Because of those restrictions, seasonal currency demands were scrambles for reserve money, which often escalated into panics.

CRITICISM OF THE FRACTIONAL RESERVE SYSTEM

Although the fractional reserve system is the only current form of banking worldwide, there is much criticism of it. According to Valkonen (2016), the reserve is fractional and does not prevent a bank run. When someone makes a deposit, he or she believes their money in the bank is safe and sound, and they can come and withdraw their money on time at any point. But in fact, only a small fraction of their money is kept in cash, while all the remaining money is lent out. If a bank gets into trouble (e.g., go bankrupt) and there's no Central Bank support, depositors will never get their money back, as a bank has nothing to give them apart from that small fraction that's kept in cash. And it's not a problem for a particular bank; it's the issue of trust in the whole banking system and, as a consequence, the country's economy as a whole. If one bank becomes insolvent, depositors may rush to other banks to withdraw their money before these other banks, too, become insolvent, and the entire system will be in trouble.

Usually, when a bank gets into trouble, it is supported by central bank finances, which give depositors the opportunity not to worry about what a bank is going to do with their funds because they will always have their money back with CB's support. With the lack of the depositors' control, banks can do whatever they want with the investments because nobody will ask where a bank intends to further invest received funds.

The government needs more money during the recession, and it may lower interest rates to motivate people to borrow and consume more and invest more. But people tend to be cautious during the recession to borrow less money than the government wants. Less borrowing leads to less borrowing, and this leads to less circulation of money. The opposite situation occurs during the boom in the economy: the government wants less money in circulation, but people tend to borrow more and spend more. More borrowing causes more borrowing. The fractional reserve system may lead to a cycle of money creation that is quite the opposite of what the economy currently needs.

In light of recent events, such as Greek default and sharpening situation in the financial sector of the Eurozone, some economists had started to blame the banking system for speculative investment behavior and the creation of financial instruments that do not improve the current economic situation (King 19 October 2011). According to King, banks should no longer assume that the general public will believe that banks know what they are doing with the investments, rates, and fees, but nowadays, the banking sector does not assume any useful social media engagement with their clients.

Banks increase the supply of money through the constant

loan-depositing process, creating money backed by nothing but debt. Considering the fact that deposits are less liquid than lending (i.e., people tend to borrow and consume more than depositing, and lending can one day exceed depositing), there is a potential risk of "demand-pull inflation" when the demand for credits exceeds the supply, and therefore the supply of money will decrease. And the decrease in the supply of money is a bad sign for the economy.

The concentration of wealth in the hands of commercial banks lets the country exist in debt, according to the Austrian economic site. People are taking loans to buy houses, cars, educate their children, etc. Some people get new loans to redeem old ones. Actually, the money is expanded through debt, in particular, through expanded personal debt. In the long run, this process is unsustainable, because debt expansion leads to artificial price growth (when people have more money in hand, they tend to consume more, and this is a good ground for market price speculation) and debt saturation, after which further debt growth is not possible and slows. This causes liquidity (as we remember, lending will exceed depositing) and brings the banks' solvency under question (Ludvig von Mises Institute 2015).

By allowing money to be made "from thin air," the fractional reserve banking causes a kind of moral hazard. In other words, the money that banks create is not backed up by physical assets and appears to be a legal way to cheat people by telling them everything they invest can be fully redeemed at any time.

PLANS TO STRENGTHEN THE BANKING SYSTEM

Today 's weakness in the US banking system stems from a different set of government policies than branching (eroded in the 1980s and finally eliminated in 1995) and banknote issue restrictions (commercial banks stopped issuing notes in the 1930s). The weakness today is not due to restrictions but due to privileges. One indication of that is that today's weakest banks are not the smallest banks but the large corporations.

Just after birth in the 1930s, federal deposit insurance has meant that a comparatively risky bank (one with less adequate capital to cover potential losses to its asset portfolio) no longer faces a tax on the retail deposit sector. Insured depositors have no incentive to shop around for a safe bank, so they no longer demand a higher rate of interest to give their deposits to it. That effectively subsidizes risk-taking.

The doctrine of 'too big to fail' compounds the problem. Even the legally uninsured depositors and subordinated debt holders are given blanket protection, removing their incentive to shop around for a prudently managed bank.

The evidence shows that when the banking system is free of hobbling legal restrictions and free of privileges, a fractional reserve banking system is not unstable. In the 19th century, the U.S. banking system was weakened by legal limits. In response to this weakness, Congress patched the issue in the 20th century by creating the Federal Reserve system (to act as a "lender of last resort") and federal deposit insurance rather than allowing the banking system to become robust by repealing its restrictions. As a result, government privileges (especially taxpayer-backed deposit insurance and taxpayer-backed "too big to fail" bailouts) that generate moral hazard chronically weakened the U.S. banking system in the 21st century. Banks take advantage of such guarantees by holding portfolios of assets that are too full of default risk and interest rate risk. They use excess leverage to finance their portfolios (too much debt, not enough equity). Rather than trying to come up with another fix, Congress would seek to dismantle the restrictions and privileges that saddled an unhealthy banking system that left the American people.

CHAPTER EIGHT

THE GREAT RECESSION OF 2007

"During the late 2000s and early 2010s, the Great Recession was a period of general economic decline observed in world markets. The recession's size and timing varied from country to country. In terms of overall impact, the International Monetary Fund concluded that this was the greatest global recession since the Second World War" (Ibrahim 1). According to the US National Bureau of Economic Research (NBER - the official arbiter of US recessions), the recession, started in December 2007 and ended in June 2009, lasting for 19 months. The Great Recession was linked to the 2007–08 financial crisis, and the 2007–09 U.S. subprime mortgage crisis.

The Great Recession of 2007 prompted the United States, by most accounts, its worst and longest recession since the Great Depression. The housing bubble began its burst; U.S. GDP started its fall into negative territory with a significant decrease in economic activity across the country. In dating recessions, the NBER considers a list of economic indicators, which include real personal income, industrial production, retail sales, non-farm employment, and GDP growth.

Owing to its severity and prolonged duration, economists dubbed it the "Great Recession," with global ramifications mostly affecting the world's advanced economies.

The Great Recession met the IMF's criteria to be a global recession, requiring a decline in real-world per capita average GDP (weighted buying power). Despite the fact that all G20 members, representing 85% of the world 's GDP, use quarterly data as recession definition criteria, the International Monetary Fund (IMF) decided – in the absence of a complete data set – not to declare/measure global recessions according to quarterly GDP figures. However, the seasonally adjusted PPP-weighted real GDP for the G20 zone is a good indicator for the world's GDP, and it was measured as having suffered a direct quarter-on-quarter decline during the three quarters from Q3-2008 to Q1-2009, which more accurately labeled the global recession.

The years leading up to the crisis have been marked by excessive growth in stock prices and subsequent boom in economic demand. Additionally, the U.S. shadow banking system (i.e., non-depository financial institutions like investment banks) had grown to compete with the depository system, but was not subject to the same regulatory oversight, making it vulnerable to a bank run. Since they provided better returns than U.S. government bonds, U.S. mortgage-backed securities were sold all over the world, despite dangers that became impossible to determine. Many of these securities were backed by subprime mortgages, which collapsed in value when the 2006 US housing bubble burst and large numbers of homeowners began defaulting on their 2007 mortgage payments.

The emergence of losses from sub-prime loans in 2007 started the crisis and exposed other risky loans and over-inflated asset prices. On the inter-bank loan market, a major panic broke out with loan losses mounting and Lehman Brothers' downfall on September 15, 2008. This was the beginning of a bank attack on the secret banking system, culminating in primary public financial aid (government bailouts), culminating in big and well-established investment and commercial banks experiencing significant losses and even collapse in the United States and Europe.

The ensuing global recession resulted in a sharp fall in international trade, rising unemployment, and falling commodity prices. Several economists predicted that recovery might not occur until 2011 and that the recession would be the worst since the 1930's Great Depression.

Governments and central banks responded with fiscal and monetary policies to boost national economies and reduce the risks to the financial system. The recession gained renewed interest in Keynesian economic ideas on how to combat recession. Economists advised that the stimulus should be withdrawn as soon as the economies recover sufficiently "to pave the way for sustainable growth."

In the United States, the allocation of household income has been more unequal during the post-2008 economic recovery, first for the US, but keeping with the trend of the past ten economic recoveries since 1949. Income inequality in the US rose in more than 2 out of 3 metropolitan areas from 2005 to 2012. Between 2005 and 2011, median household wealth fell 35% in the US, from $106,591 to $68,839.

CAUSES OF THE GREAT RECESSION
Panel reports

In January 2011, the Financial Crisis Investigation Committee (FCIC), composed of six Democrats and four Republican appointees, announced its conclusions. It concluded that "the recession could have been prevented and was triggered by: systemic financial regulatory weaknesses, including the Federal Reserve 's inability to curb the flow of toxic mortgages; drastic breakdowns in corporate governance, with too many irresponsible and risk-taking financial firms; and an unsustainable combination of excessive household and Wall Street funding."

There were two FCIC reports of Republican dissent. One of them, signed by three Republican candidates, concluded that multiple causes exist. In his separate dissent to the FCIC's majority and minority views, American Enterprise Institute (AEI) Commissioner Peter J. Wallison primarily blamed the crisis to US housing policy, including Fannie & Freddie's actions. He wrote: "When the bubble started to deflate in mid-2007, unprecedented numbers of the low-quality and high-risk loans created by government policies failed.

The group of 20 leaders cited the following causes in their "Declaration of the Summit on Financial Markets and the World Economy" of 15 November 2008: during a period of strong global growth, increasing capital flows and prolonged stability earlier this decade, market participants sought higher yields without adequate risk appreciation and failed to exercise due diligence.

Narratives

Several "narratives" attempt to analyze the causes of the recession with overlapping elements:

1. The inverse of a bank run on the shadow banking network, which comprises investment banks and other non-depository financial institutions, had evolved to contend on a scale with the depository network but had not yet been exposed to the same regulatory protections.

2. The US economy was driven by a housing bubble, and as it burst, private residential investment (i.e., housing construction) fell by nearly 4% of GDP, and consumption enabled by bubble-generated housing wealth also slowed, creating an annual demand gap of almost $1 trillion.

3. High levels of household debt accumulated in the decades preceding the crisis resulted in a balance sheet recession (similar to debt deflation) after housing prices began to decline in 2006. Consumers started paying off debt, which reduced their consumption, slowing the economy for an extended period as debt levels

decreased.

4. US government policies encouraged home ownership even for those who couldn't afford it, contributing to lax lending standards, unsustainable increases in household prices, and indebtedness. There is also an underlying theory that rising income disparities and wage inflation motivated households to increase their household debt in order to sustain their ideal standard of life which further fueled the bubble. Also, this more significant share of income flowing to the top increased the political power of business interests, which utilized that power to deregulate or limit shadow banking system regulation.

Trade imbalances and debt bubbles

In July 2012, The Economist reported that the surge of investment dollars required to fund the US trade deficit was a big trigger of the housing bubble and financial crisis: "Trade deficit in the early 1990s was less than 1% of GDP, and in 2006 it hit 6%."

Foreign savings, notably from East Asia and the Middle East, much of that money went to dodgy mortgages to buy overvalued houses, and the result was a financial crisis.

In February 2012, describing the crisis in Europe, Paul Krugman wrote that: "What we are essentially looking at, then, is a balance of payments problem, in which capital flooded south after the euro was formed, leading to overvaluation in southern Europe."

Monetary policy

Another narrative on the origin focused on the respective parts of public monetary policy (especially in the US) and private financial institutions' practices. In the U.S., mortgage funding was unusually decentralized, opaque, and competitive, and competition between income lenders and market share is believed to have led to a decline in underwriting standards and risky lending.

Although the role of Alan Greenspan as Chairman of the Federal Reserve has been widely discussed, the main point of controversy remains the reduction of the Federal Funds rate to 1% for more than a year, which, according to Austrian theorists, has injected enormous amounts of "easy" credit-based money into the financial system and created an unsustainable economic boom.

High private debt levels

Another narrative focuses on high private debt levels within the US economy. At the end of 2007, US household debt as a percentage of annual disposable personal income was 127%, compared with 77% in 1990. As their adjustable mortgage payments rose, households began to default in record numbers, rendering mortgage-backed securities worthless. High levels of private debt also impacted growth by deepening recessions and weakening the recovery that follows. Robert Reich claims that the amount of debt in the US economy can be traced to economic inequality, assuming middle-class wages stagnated while wealth concentrated at the top, and households "pull equity out of their homes and overload debt in order to maintain living standards."

In April 2012, the IMF reported: "Household debt soared in the years leading up to the downturn. In advanced economies, the debt-to-income ratio rose by an average of 39% to 138% in the five years preceding 2007. In Denmark, Iceland, Ireland, the Netherlands, and Norway, debt peaked at over 200% of household income.

When house prices plummeted, leading to the global financial crisis, many households saw their wealth shrink due to their debt, and with declining incomes and more unemployment, found it more difficult to meet mortgage payments. By the end of 2011, real house prices in Ireland had fallen by about 41%, in Iceland by 29%, in Spain and the USA by 23%, and in Denmark by 21%. Household defaults, distressed mortgages (which surpass the house valuation of the debt balance), foreclosures, and fire selling became common across a variety of economies. In some countries, household deleveraging started by paying off debts or defaulting on them. It was most pronounced in the U.S., where around two-thirds of debt reduction reflected defaults.

Pre-recession economic imbalances

The onset of the economic crisis was a surprise for most people. A 2009 report names twelve analysts and pundits who forecasted a U.S. recession between 2000 and 2006, focused on the fall of the then-thriving housing market: Wynne Godley, Eric Janszen, Steve Keen, Jens Kjaer Sørensen, Dean Baker, Kurt Richebächer, Fred Harrison, Nouriel Roubini, Michael Hudson, Peter Schiff, Jakob Brøchner Madsen, and Robert Shiller.

Housing bubbles

By 2007, in many parts of the world, real estate bubbles were still underway, especially in the United States, France, United Kingdom, Spain, Netherlands, Australia, United Arab Emirates, New Zealand, Ireland, Poland, South Africa, Greece, Bulgaria, Croatia, Norway, Singapore, South Korea, Sweden, Finland, Argentina, the Baltic States, India, Romania, Ukraine, and China. In mid-2005, U.S. Federal Reserve Chairman Alan Greenspan said that "at least there's a little 'froth' [on the U.S. housing market]...it's hard not to see that there's a lot of local bubbles."

Writing at the same time, the Economist newspaper went further, saying, "the worldwide rise in house prices is the biggest bubble in history." Real estate bubbles are (by interpretation of the term "bubble") accompanied by a market drop (also regarded as a house price crash) that may result in certain investors having negative equity (a mortgage loan higher than the property's current value).

Increases in uncertainty

Increases in uncertainty depresses investment or consumption, and the 2007–14 recession is the most striking episode since 1960 with elevated uncertainty.

Inappropriate or Ineffective regulation
Regulations encouraging lax lending standards

Several experts, such as the American Enterprise Institute's Peter Wallison and Edward Pinto, have reported that private borrowers are being forced to loosen lending conditions by affordable housing initiatives by government. They reference the 1992 Housing and Economic Development Act, which initially mandated 30% or more of Fannie and Freddie's loan transactions to be linked to suitable housing. The legislation gave Department of Housing and Urban Development (HUD) the power to set future requirements, and ultimately at least 56% was established (under the Bush administration). Fannie Mae and Freddie Mac developed schemes to purchase $5 trillion in affordable housing loans to fulfill the criteria, and urged borrowers to loosen underwriting standards to produce such loans.

The Republican Minority Dissenting Report of the FCIC also concluded that US housing policies were not a robust explanation for a broader global housing bubble. The view that U.S. housing policies were the primary cause of the crisis was widely disputed, with Paul Krugman referring to them as "imaginary history."

Derivatives

Author Michael Lewis wrote that a credit default swap (CDS) form of derivative allowed speculators to stake bets on the same mortgage securities. Speculators who bought CDS protection wagered that significant defaults in mortgage security would occur, while sellers (such as AIG) bet that they would not. When massive defaults on underlying mortgage securities occurred, companies like AIG that sold CDS were unable to fulfill and defaulted on their side of the obligation; U.S. taxpayers paid more than $100 billion to global financial institutions to honor AIG obligations, generating considerable outrage.

Derivatives like CDS were unregulated or barely regulated. Several sources also noted the US government's failure to oversee derivatives. In 1998, Brooksley E. Born, Chief of the Commodity Futures Trading Commission, released a policy paper demanding feedback from regulators, lobbyists, policymakers about how derivatives should be registered, traded via a central system or whether capital standards would be expected from their purchasers. Greenspan, Rubin, and Levitt urged her to remove the paper, and Greenspan convinced Congress to pass a bill that would prohibit CFTC from controlling derivatives for another six months — when Born's term of office ended. In the end, it was the collapse of a particular type of derivative, mortgage-backed security that triggered the economic crisis of 2008.

Shadow banking system

In 2009, Paul Krugman wrote that the shadow banking system was the "core of what happened" that caused the crisis. As the shadow banking system expanded to equal or perhaps exceeded the importance of conventional banking, policymakers and policy officials should have known they were recreating the sort of financial instability that rendered the Great Depression inevitable – so they should have reacted by expanding legislation and the financial security net to protect all emerging institutions.

Three of America's largest investment banks all went bankrupt during 2008 (Lehman Brothers) or were sold to other banks (Bear Stearns and Merrill Lynch) at fire-sale prices. Investment banks were not subject to the stricter rules that applied to depository banks. These failures exacerbated global financial system instability.

The other two investment banks, Morgan Stanley and Goldman Sachs, experiencing imminent collapse, decided to become commercial banks, thus subjecting themselves to stricter regulation but receiving credit access via the Federal Reserve. Furthermore, as debtors defaulted on these securities, American Industrial Group (AIG) had insured mortgage-backed securities and other loans but was not entitled to retain enough reserves to meet its obligations. AIG was contractually required to post extra collateral with many creditors and counterparties, causing controversy when more than $100 billion in U.S. taxpayer money was distributed on behalf of AIG to major global financial institutions. Though AIG legitimately owes this money to the banks (under agreements signed by the institutions through credit default swaps purchased from AIG), a number of Congressmen and members of the media expressed outrage at the use of taxpayer money to bail out banks.

Economist Gary Gorton wrote in May 2009: "Unlike previous 19th and early 20th-century financial panics, the present banking crisis is a wholesale crisis, not a market panic." In earlier episodes, depositors ran to their banks and demanded cash in exchange for their checking accounts.

The Financial Crisis Investigation Commission concluded in January 2011: "We established a number of safeguards in the early part of the 20th century – the Federal Reserve as a last resort lender, federal deposit insurance, robust legislation – to include a bulwark against the panics that frequently threatened America's banking sector throughout the 20th century. However, we have allowed the growth over the past 30-plus years of a shadow banking system – opaque and laden with short-term debt – that rivaled the size of the traditional banking system. Primary market components – for example, the multi-trillion-dollar lending market, off-balance-sheet entities, and the usage of over-the-counter derivatives – remain shielded from view without the protections that we had built to deter financial turmoil. We had a financial system of the 21st century with safeguards of the 19th century."

Systemic crisis

A number of economists have described the financial crisis and recession as a symptom of yet another, more profound crisis. For example, Ravi Batra claims that that financial capitalism injustice creates investment bubbles that burst, causing depression and significant political changes. Feminist economists Ailsa McKay and Margunn Bjørnholt claim that the financial crisis and the reaction to it exposed a lack of ideas in mainstream economics and in the economics profession, arguing for a reorganization of both the government, economic theory, and economics. Such reorganization they say should include new advances in feminist economics and ecological economics that take the socially responsible, sensitive and accountable subject as their starting point in creating an economy and economic theories that fully recognize each other and the planet.

EFFECTS OF THE GREAT RECESSION
Effects on the United States

Until December 2012, persistent high unemployment in the U.S. remained, along with low consumer morale, continuing decline in home values and increased foreclosures and personal bankruptcies, increasing federal debt, inflation, and rising petroleum and food prices. A 2011 poll found that over half of all Americans thought the United States continued to be in recession or even depression, although economic data displayed a modest recovery.

- In the third quarter of 2008, actual gross domestic product (GDP) began contracting and grew only in Q1 2010. In February 2013, the Congressional Budget Office (CBO) estimated that the real U.S. GDP remained just over 4.5%, or about $850 billion, above its previous peak. CBO expected GDP not to return to its potential level until 2017. The US GDP in 2009 stood at $14.4 trillion. The US GDP had grown by 18.6%, equal to $17.7 trillion, by the final quarter of 2014. Canada, the largest trading partner in the United States at that time, had a GDP of $1.37 trillion in 2009, but reached $2 trillion by 2014, increasing by more than 31%. Both countries now have the fastest rising economies in the G8 and G20, and both countries have increased each other's daily exchange from $1.5 trillion in 2011 to $4 trillion in 2014, representing more than $1.3 trillion in annual trade.

- The unemployment rate increased to 5% in the pre-crisis period in 2008 to 10% by the end of 2009, then steadily declined to 7.3% by March 2013. The number of unemployed rose from about 7 million in pre-crisis 2008 to 15 million by 2009, then dropped to 12 million by early 2013.

- Private residential investment (mainly housing) fell from

its pre-crisis high of $800 billion in 2006 to $400 billion by mid-2009 and stayed depressed at that level. Non-residential investment (mainly business capital equipment purchases) peaked at $1.7 trillion in pre-crisis 2008 and dropped to $1.3 trillion in 2010 but had almost recovered to this peak by early 2013.

- Housing prices fell by about 30% on average from their high of mid-2006 to mid-2009 and remained at about that level as of March 2013.

- As measured by the S&P 500 index, stock market prices dropped from their peak of 1,565 in October 2007 to 676 in March 2009, down 57%. Stock prices then began a slow rise and recovered to record highs by April 2013.

- The net worth of U.S. households and non-profits fell from around $67 trillion in 2007 to $52 trillion in 2009, down $15 trillion or 22% in 2009. It started to recover afterward and stood at $66 trillion by Q3 2012.

- The total US national debt rose from 66% of GDP in pre-crisis 2008 to more than 103% by the end of 2012.

- For the most part, income levels dropped significantly, with the average male worker making $32,137 in 2010. In comparison, an average male worker was making an inflation-adjusted income of $32,844 in 1968. The 2007–2009 recession is deemed to be the worst downturn since the Great Depression. And one of the worst in the subsequent economic recovery. Since 2000, the weak economic performance has seen the percentage of working-age adults employed drop from 64% to 58%

(a number last seen in 1984).

- Federal disability rolls have been added to approximately 5.4 million people as discouraged workers quit their quest for jobs and take benefit of the Federal System.

- United States has seen growing accumulation of capital at the cost of the middle class and the disadvantaged. The middle class dropped to 51% in 2011, from 61% of the population in 1971, while the upper class increased its stake in national income from 29% in 1970 to 46% in 2010. The share for the middle class fell to 45% from 62%, while the total revenue for the poor fell from 10% to 9%. Since the number of poor has increased during this period, the smaller piece of the pie is spread over a more significant portion of the population (down to 9% from 10%). The part of national capital held by the middle class and the poor has also declined as their share of national income has fallen, rendering it harder to accumulate wealth.

- The younger generation, which would just begin their accumulation of wealth, were hit the hardest. Those that are under 35 are 68% less affluent than they were in 1984, whereas those who are over 55 are 10% wealthier. Much of that concentration has taken place since the beginning of the Great Recession. In 2009, 87.2% of all wealth was controlled by the most affluent 20% households, up from 85.0% in 2007. 35.6% of all wealth was controlled by the top 1%, up from 34.6% in 2007. The share of the lowest 80% dropped from 15% to

12.8%, falling 15%.

- Inflation-adjusted mean household income in the United States stood at $53,252 (at the height of the Internet bubble). In 1999, the number fell to $51,174 in 2004, increased to 52,823 in 2007 (at the height of the housing bubble) and since then has sunk to $49,445 in 2010. The last time median household income was at this level in 1996 was $49,112, indicating that the early 2000 recession and global recession of 2008–2012 have wiped out all profit of the middle class for the last 15 years. This drop in income has caused a dramatic rise in people living below the level of poverty and has particularly hit the suburbs.

- Between 2000 and 2010, the number of affluent households below the poverty line rose by 53%, relative to a rise of 23% in urban poor households. A 2011 poll found that, despite official data showing a historically modest recovery, over half of all Americans believe the US is still in recession, or even depression. The poverty rate defined by the Census Bureau decreased to about 14.5% of the population in 2013. A majority of Americans still believed the nation remained in a recession as late as 2014 and early 2015.

Effects on Europe

Europe's crisis has generally advanced from banking system crises to sovereign debt crises, as many countries chose to bail out their banking systems using taxpayer money. Greece was different in that its banking system faced large public debts rather than problems. Several countries issued "troika" bailout packages (European Central Bank, International Monetary Fund, and European Commission) implementing a number of emergency measures as well.

Many countries in Europe embarked on austerity initiatives, reducing their budget deficits from 2010 to 2011 in relation to GDP. For instance, Greece reduced its budget deficit from 10.4% of GDP in 2010 to 9.6% in 2011, according to the CIA World Factbook. Iceland, Italy, Ireland, Portugal, France, and Spain have also improved their budget deficits in relation to GDP from 2010 to 2011.

However, most of these countries, with the exception of Germany, had public-debt-to-GDP levels, which increased (i.e., deteriorated) from 2010 to 2011. The Greek debt-to-GDP ratio rose from 143% in 2010 to 165% in 2011 to 185% in 2014. This indicates that GDP growth during this time, given reducing budget deficits, was not adequate to sustain a decline (improvement) in the debt-to-GDP ratio for these countries. Eurostat announced that in 2008 the debt-to-GDP level for the 17 euro area countries was 70.1%, in 2009 it was 79.9%, in 2010 it was 85.3%, and in 2011 it was 87.2%.

In Spain, Greece, Italy, Ireland, Portugal, and the United Kingdom, the unemployment rate in 2011 fell, according to the CIA World Factbook. France saw no significant changes, while unemployment levels decreased in Germany and Iceland. In September 2012, Eurostat reported that unemployment in the Eurozone reached record levels of 11.6%, up from 10.3% the previous year.

Though, unemployment differed considerably by region. Economist Martin Wolf analyzed during April 2012 the relationship between cumulative GDP growth from 2008-2012 and total deficit reduction due to austerity policies in several European countries (see chart to the right). He concluded: "In general, there is little indication here that big fiscal contractions [reduction of budget deficits] offer optimism and development gains that outweigh the direct consequences of contractions, delivering exactly what one might expect: small contractions offer recessions, and major contractions bring depressions."

In April 2012, Economist Paul Krugman analyzed the relationship between GDP and a reduction in budget deficits for many European countries and concluded that, according to Martin Wolf, austerity was slowing growth. He also wrote: "...this also implies that 1 euro of austerity yields a reduced deficit of only about 0.4 euros, even in the short run. No wonder, then, that the entire austerity enterprise is spiraling into disaster."

Countries that avoided recession

Poland and Slovakia are the only two leaders of the European Union in the years impacted by the Great Recession to have avoided a GDP recession. The Polish economy had not entered recession or even contracted as of December 2009. Analysts identified several causes of positive economic development in Poland: extremely low levels of bank loans and a relatively small mortgage market; the relatively recent dismantling of EU trade barriers and the resulting increase in demand for Polish goods since 2004; receiving direct EU funding since 2004; and lack of over-dependence on a single export sector.

While India, Uzbekistan, China, and Iran experienced slow growth at the time, they did not enter recessions. In the first quarter of 2009, South Korea narrowly avoided a technical recession. In mid-September, the International Energy Agency stated that for the whole of 2009, South Korea could be the only large OECD country to avoid recession. In the first half of 2009, it was the only developed economy to expand.

After experiencing only one-quarter of negative growth in the fourth quarter of 2008, Australia avoided a technical recession, with GDP gaining back positive in the first quarter of 2009. The financial crisis has, to a great extent, not impacted developing countries. Experts see many reasons: Because it is not fully integrated into the world market. For example, Africa was not affected during the time, as they had experienced crises before, and Latin America and Asia seemed better prepared.

Policy responses

In many national financial systems, the financial phase of the crisis has led to emergency interventions. As the crisis in many major economies developed into a genuine recession, economic stimulus meant to revive economic growth became the most common national policy. After the rescue plans for the banking system were implemented, major developed and emerging countries announced plans to relieve their economies. Economic stimulus plans were announced, especially in Europe, the United States, and the European Union. The financial crisis in the final quarter of 2008 saw the G-20 group of major economies assume a new significance as a focus for handling the economic and financial crisis.

United States policy responses

The Federal Reserve, Treasury, and the Securities & Exchange Commission took several steps to intervene in the crisis on September 19. The Treasury also announced a new $50 billion investment insurance program on September 19 to halt the potential run on money market mutual funds, similar to the Federal Deposit Insurance Corporation (FDIC) program. Part of the notices contained provisional exceptions from section 23A and section 23B (Regulation W), which allowed financial groups to share funds more efficiently within their group. The exceptions would end on 30 January 2009 unless the Federal Reserve Board extended them. As part of its reaction to the mortgage crisis, the Securities and Exchange Commission announced an end to short-selling of 799 financial stocks, as well as action against naked short-selling. In May 2013, as the stock market hit record highs and the housing and employment markets improved slightly, the Federal Reserve's prospect of beginning to decrease its economic stimulus activities began to enter investment analysts' projections and affected global markets.

Asia-Pacific policy responses

China slashed its interest rate for the first time since 2002 on September 15, 2008. Indonesia reduced its overnight repo rate, at which commercial banks can borrow central bank funds overnight by two percentage points to 10.25%. Australia's Reserve Bank injected nearly $ 1.5 billion into the banking system, almost three times the estimated requirement on the market. India's Reserve Bank added nearly $1.32 billion through a repayment operation.

The Chinese policy support package, on 9 November 2008, was a stimulus package of RMB 4 trillion ($586 billion), announced by the People's Republic of China's central government in its big push to save the global financial crisis from affecting the second-largest economy in the world.

A statement on the government website said a plan to invest 4 trillion yuan ($586 billion) in social welfare and infrastructure by the end of 2010, was approved by the State Council. The stimulus package invested in critical areas such as housing, rural infrastructure, transportation, health and education, environment, industry, rebuilding disasters, income building, tax cuts, and finance. China's export-driven economy began to feel the impact of the US and European economic slowdown, and in less than two months the government lowered core interest rates three times in an effort to stimulate economic development. On 28 November 2008, the Ministry of Finance of the People's Republic of China and the State Tax Administration jointly announced an increase in the rate of export tax rebates on certain labor-intensive goods.

World leaders and analysts welcomed the stimulus package as more substantial than expected and a sign that China is helping to stabilize the global economy by boosting its own economy. Marc Faber claimed, however, that on January 16 2009, he thought China was still in recession.

In Taiwan, the central bank announced it would slash its required reserve ratios for the first time in eight years on

September 16, 2008. On the same day, the central bank added $3.59 billion to the interbank foreign-currency market. Bank of Japan pumped $29.3bn into the financial system on September 17, 2008, and Australia's Reserve Bank added $3.45bn the same day.

Response to global crisis in developing and emerging economies consisted mainly of low-rates monetary policy (mainly Asia and the Middle East) coupled with currency depreciation against the dollar. In the Middle East, in Argentina, and in some Asian countries, stimulus plans were also in place. In Asia, plans generally amounted to 1-3% of GDP, with the notable exception of China, which announced a plan that accounted for 16% of GDP.

European policy responses

The European policy measures were confined to a limited number of countries (Spain and Italy) until September 2008. The measures in both countries were devoted to reforming the household tax system (tax rebates) in support of specific sectors such as housing.

Fortis was partially nationalized on 29 September 2008 by the Belgian, Luxembourg and Dutch authorities. Hypo Real Estate was bailed out by the German Government. The British Government announced a stimulus package on 8 October 2008 for the bank of around £500 billion (at the time $850 billion). The plan had three parts to it. The first £200 billion in liquidity stack would be made in respect of the banks. The second part will consist of increasing the capital market within banks by the state government. Along with that, if the banks needed it, £50bn will be made available. Finally, the government will write off any eligible loans between British banks with a £250bn limit.

German finance minister at the time Peer Steinbrück indicated in early December a lack of belief in a "Great Rescue Plan" and a reluctance to spend more money on the crisis. In March 2009, the Presidency of the European Union confirmed that the EU at the time strongly resisted the pressure from the US to increase European budget deficits.

From 2010, the UK began a fiscal consolidation program to reduce debt and deficit levels while stimulating economic recovery at the same time. Other European countries also started fiscal consolidation, with similar goals.

Global responses

A first crisis-dedicated summit was held in November 2008 at the Heads of State level (G20 Washington Summit 2008). The G-20 countries met at a summit held in Washington in November 2008 to address the economic crisis. In addition to proposals on international financial regulation, they pledged to take measures to support and coordinate their economy and denied any resort to protectionism.

In April 2009, a further G-20 Summit was held in London. In March, finance ministers and G-20 leaders of central banks met in Horsham, England, to prepare for the meeting pledged to boost economic prosperity. They agreed to organize their actions and to increase competition and jobs. They also pledged to combat all forms of protectionism and to maintain trade and foreign investment.

They also committed to maintaining credit supply by providing more liquidity and recapitalizing the banking system, and to implementing stimulus plans quickly. As for central banks, they pledged to maintain policy at low rates as long as needed. Finally, through the strengthening of the IMF, the leaders decided to help emerging and developing countries.

CHAPTER NINE

THE BIRTH OF BITCOIN

What is Bitcoin?

According to Frankenfield, Bitcoin is a digital currency created after the housing-market crash in January 2009 (Jake Frankenfield). It follows the ideas of the mysterious and pseudonymous Satoshi Nakamoto set out in a whitepaper. The identity of the person or peoples responsible for creating the technology remains unknown. Bitcoin offers lower transaction costs than traditional online payment mechanisms and is operated by a decentralized body, unlike currencies controlled by the government.

There are no physical bitcoins; only balance on a public

ledger is maintained, and everyone has transparent access, which is verified by a massive amount of computing power – along with all Bitcoin transactions. No banks or governments issue or back Bitcoins, nor are individual Bitcoins valuable as merchandise. Although it is was not a legal tender at the time, Bitcoin became highly popular over the years and has collectively triggered hundreds of other virtual currencies called Altcoins.

UNDERSTANDING BITCOIN

Bitcoin is a collection of computers, or nodes, which all run the code of Bitcoin and store their blockchain. One could think of a blockchain as a collection of blocks. There is a collection of transactions within each block. Because all of these blockchain-running computers have the same list of blocks and transactions and can see these new blocks filled with new Bitcoin transactions transparently, no one can cheat the system. Anyone, whether or not they run a "node" to Bitcoin, can watch these transactions happen live. To achieve a nefarious act, 51% of the computing power that makes up Bitcoin would need to be operated by a bad actor. Currently, Bitcoin has over 10,000 nodes, and this number is increasing, making such an attack quite unlikely.

In the event of an attack, the Bitcoin nodes, or the people who take part with their computer in the Bitcoin network, would likely fork into a new blockchain making the effort put forth by the bad actor to achieve a waste of the attack.

Bitcoin tokens balances are kept using both public and private "keys," which are long strings of numbers and letters linked by the mathematical encryption that was created with an algorithm. The public key (comparable to a bank account number) is the address that is released to the world and can be submitted to bitcoins by others. The private key (as opposed to an ATM PIN) is intended as a guarded secret and is only used to allow transmissions from Bitcoin. Bitcoin keys cannot be mistaken with a Bitcoin wallet, which is a physical or digital device that facilitates Bitcoin trading and will enable users to monitor coin ownership. The term "wallet" is a bit misleading since the decentralized nature of Bitcoin means that it is never stored "in" a wallet, but preferably on a blockchain in a decentralized state.

The term "Bitcoin" is capitalized by reference to the entity or concept, according to the official Bitcoin Foundation, whereas "bitcoin" is written in the lower case by reference to a quantity of the currency (e.g. "I traded 20 bitcoin") or the units themselves. The plural type may be just "cash" or "bitcoins." Bitcoin is commonly referred to as "BTC" as well.

HOW BITCOIN BEGAN

18 August 2008: Bitcoin.org was registered as a domain name.

31 October 2008: A person or group using the name Satoshi Nakamoto makes an announcement on metzdowd.com's The Cryptography Mailing List: "I've been working on a new, fully peer-to-peer electronic cash system, with no third party to trust. The paper can be found at http:/www.bitcoin.org/bitcoin.pdf. "This link takes you to the now popular whitepaper. Entitled 'Bitcoin: A Peer-to-Peer Electronic Cash System' published on

bitcoin.org. This paper would become the primary leader in how Bitcoin operates today.

3 January 2009, the first Bitcoin block mining, Block 0, was created. This is also regarded as the "genesis block" and includes the following text: "03/Jan/2009 Chancellor on the verge of second rescue for banks," maybe as proof that the stone was extracted on or around that date, and perhaps also as crucial political statement. January 8, 2009: The first version of the Bitcoin program is distributed on The Cryptography Mailing List. 9 January 2009: Block 1 is mined, and Bitcoin mining is seriously starting.

Who is Responsible for the Invention of Bitcoin?

Nobody knows who introduced Bitcoin, or at least not conclusively. However, Satoshi Nakamoto is the name associated with the person or group of people who published the original 2008 Bitcoin white paper and worked on the original 2009 Bitcoin software. Many individuals have reported to be or were proposed as the real-life people behind the alias in the years after that period, but as of May 2020, the true identity (or identities) behind Satoshi remains obscured.

While it is enticing to accept the spin of the media that Satoshi Nakamoto is a solitary, quixotic genius who developed Bitcoin from thin air, these inventions usually do not exist in a vacuum. All the major scientific discoveries were built on previously existing research. Bitcoin has precursors: Adam Back's Hashcash, invented in 1997, and then Wei Dai 's b-money, Nick Szabo's gold piece, and Hal Finney's Reusable Work Proof. The Bitcoin whitepaper itself cites Hashcash and b-money, as well as numerous other works spanning several research fields. Perhaps unsurprisingly, it was suspected that many of the individuals behind the other projects mentioned above had had a part to play in developing Bitcoin.

Why Isn't Satoshi Known?

There are a few motivations for the inventor of Bitcoin to keep the secret of his or her identity. One is confidentiality. Since Bitcoin has gained popularity – becoming something of a worldwide phenomenon – it is likely that Satoshi Nakamoto would attract a lot of media and government attention.

Another reason might be the Bitcoin's potential to cause major disruption to current banking and monetary systems. If Bitcoin achieved mass adoption, the system could exceed the sovereign fiat currencies of nations. This threat to existing currency might motivate governments to take legal action against the creator of Bitcoin.

The other reason for doing so is safety. In 2009 alone, 32,489 blocks were extracted; the total 2009 payout was 1,624,500 Bitcoins at a rate of 50 Bitcoins per block at that time, which at December 17, 2017, amounted to $32.14 billion. One may conclude that, through 2009, only Satoshi and perhaps a few others were mining and wielded a majority of that BTC stash. Someone in possession of so much bitcoin could become a target of criminals, particularly since bitcoins seem less like securities and more like money, in which the private keys needed to approve spending could be printed out and simply kept under a mattress. While it is likely that the inventor of Bitcoin would be taking precautions to trace any transfers induced by extortion, remaining anonymous is the right way for Satoshi to limit exposure.

HOW BITCOIN WORKS

Bitcoin is the first digital currency to use peer-to-peer technology to facilitate instant payments and popularize it. The autonomous entities and companies that control the processing resources and operate in the Bitcoin network are comprised of nodes or miners. "Miners" are attracted by the incentives (new bitcoin release) and the transaction fees charged in bitcoin, or the people on the blockchain that process the transactions. One can see these miners as the decentralized authority that enforces the Bitcoin network's credibility. New bitcoin is being released at a fixed, but periodically declining rate to the miners, so that the total bitcoin supply approaches 21 million. There are currently roughly 3 million bitcoins that still need to be mined. In this sense, Bitcoin (and any cryptocurrency generated by a similar process) works differently from fiat currency; in centralized banking systems, funds are released at a pace that suits the growth of goods in an attempt to maintain market stability, while a decentralized system like Bitcoin sets the release rate in advance and in accordance with an algorithm.

Bitcoin mining is the process that releases the bitcoins into circulation. Mining generally requires the solving of computationally difficult puzzles to discover a new block that is included in the blockchain. Mining adds and verifies records of transactions across the network, contributing to the blockchain. Miners get a bonus in the form of a few bitcoins to add blocks to the blockchain; the reward is halved every 210,000 blocks. The block reward in 2009 was 50 new bitcoins and is 6.25 as of May

2020. Bitcoin can be mined by a variety of hardware, but some yield higher rewards than others. More rewards can be achieved by certain computer chips called Application-Specific Integrated Circuits (ASIC) and by more advanced processing units such as Graphics Processing Units (GPU) These sophisticated mining processors are called "mining rigs."

One bitcoin can be divided into eight decimal places (100 millionths of a bitcoin), and this smallest unit is called a Satoshi. If necessary, and if the change is accepted by the participating miners, Bitcoin could eventually be divided into even more decimals.

Bitcoin as a Means of Payment

Bitcoins may be accepted as a method of payment for products sold or services made available. If you have a brick and mortar store, simply display a sign saying "Bitcoin Accepted Here," and many of your customers might well take you on it; transactions can be handled with the required hardware terminal or wallet address via QR codes and touch screen applications. An online business can accept bitcoins easily by simply adding this payment option to its other credit cards, PayPal, etc..

Bitcoin as an Investment

There are a lot of Bitcoin supporters who believe the future is digital currency. Many of those who endorse Bitcoin believe it facilitates a much faster, low-fee transaction payment system across the globe. Although there is very little support from government or central bank, Bitcoin can be traded for conventional currencies. Also, one of the main reasons for the growth of digital currencies such as Bitcoin is that they can act as an alternative to national fiat money and conventional goods and services such as gold.

The IRS stated in March 2014 that all virtual assets, including bitcoins, will be treated as property rather than cash. Bitcoin gains or losses held as capital will be realized as capital gains or losses while Bitcoins stored as inventory will incur ordinary gains or losses. Examples of transactions that can be taxed are selling bitcoins you mined or bought from another party or using bitcoins to pay for goods or services.

Buying on a Bitcoin exchange is the most popular way to build up the currency, but there are many other ways to earn and own bitcoins.

The Risk Involved

Although Bitcoin was not designed as a regular investment in equity (no shares were issued), some speculative investors were drawn to the digital money after it rapidly appreciated in May 2011 and again in November 2013. Thus, many people buy bitcoin, not as a medium of exchange but for its investment thesis.

Its lack of guaranteed value and digital nature; however, means buying and using bitcoins carries several inherent risks. Investors have received numerous alerts from the Securities and Exchange Commission (SEC), the Financial Industry Regulatory Authority (FINRA), the Consumer Financial Protection Bureau (CFPB), and other agencies.

The virtual currency concept is still novel, and Bitcoin doesn't have much of a long-term track record or credit history to back it up compared with traditional investments. Bitcoins are becoming less experimental every day with their increasing popularity, yet they (like all digital currencies) remain in a development phase after eleven years and are continually evolving. "It's perhaps the highest-risk, highest-return investment you can make," says Barry Silbert, Digital Currency Group CEO, which builds and invests in Bitcoin and blockchain companies.

CHAPTER TEN

EVOLUTION OF BITCOIN AND CRYPTOCURRENCIES

The Complex History of Cryptocurrency

The prevalence of cryptocurrency has hit an all-time high in our society. From a whispered commodity to a fully orchestrated, functioning system stacked with multiple competing markets and companies—it seems definitive now, that this once novel form of digital currency, is here to stay.

To further that assessment, Bitcoin, perhaps the most well-known figurehead of the cryptocurrency market broke its own recorded record, of value per coin, by exceeding $41k on

January 4th, 2021. While we have long since passed the crypto-frenzy that turned the economic world upside down—the one that saw the meager investment sums of hopeful investors skyrocket as Bitcoin exploded onto the mainstage—it hasn't stopped the yearly rising interest in cryptocurrency.

As Bitcoin reigns the undisputed champion, investors still search far and wide for the next up-and-coming contender to, once again, catch that lightning in a bottle and become the 'next' Bitcoin.

However, it is impossible to overstate just how important the effect Bitcoin has had on digital money and cryptocurrency as a whole. Its sudden surge in 2017 set the world alight in research of the cryptocurrency market. Media outlets, interest groups and monstrous amounts of would-be millionaires suddenly set about to make their claim in this new economic phenomenon. Since those years cryptocurrency has only increased in popularity, marketability, and new companies are still popping up everywhere—so it's safe to say that this innovative business model isn't going anywhere.

Although, cryptocurrency and its staying power will only be fully cemented by legal means—as in Bermuda, that structured a functioning model to domicile initial coin offerings (ICOs) for nearly two billion citizens that previously did without traditional bank accounts. Their innovative push allowed cryptocurrency to be elevated to the mainstream and used for everyday transactions through smartphones. With that figure in mind, the global market has 1.7 billion individuals without access to a bank and yet two-thirds of that number have a mobile phone. A solution lies in waiting.

But to understand that solution, it's important to key into the history of cryptocurrency by defining what it is, how it was formed, what inspired its inception, and where it's headed next.

What is Cryptocurrency?

To put it simply, cryptocurrencies are a form of digital money that are created by using encryption-based technology to program software. The money, or coin is generated within a domain that links together a peer-to-peer computer network. With that in mind, these digital domains are kept secure through a distributed, unassailable database known as a block-chain. The blockchain serves as the primary accounting system by which all transactions are kept accounted for. In other words, an official, digital record book. Further, to verify the authenticity of all these transactions, the database network implements a consensus model. A fault-tolerant system that allows for data to achieve necessary agreement without a singular administrator running the database.

A Decentralized System

The thing that makes this entire system unique is that, unlike a traditional centralized financial system, cryptocurrency decentralizes the entire system of accounting. With the use of the consensus mechanism, safety is the number one priority as the model (based on cryptography and the implementation of unique digital signatures) uses public as well as private keys, along with complex algorithms to make sure no singular entity has unrestricted access. The system works on a shared, peer-to-peer network of computers and miners that operate on open-sourced software to perform, for lack of a better term, 'research', in an attempt to verify and permanently record transactions to a publicly accessed network which can be viewed in the network.

This complex method of decentralized safety assuages the skeptical nature of participants who, though may be strangers to one another on a shared ledger, are connected by a transactional validation process. All the being said, this model allows the simple transfer of ownership of property and funds without the need for a trusted, centralized intermediary system, as is common with our everyday financial services. The incredible feat of mathematics, encryption, and engineering necessary to create such a platform, though infinitely complex and yet still remarkably safe, deserve a round of applause for laying this groundwork upon which future innovations can be implemented.

The Less than Famous Origin

While Bitcoin may be the first cryptocurrency to garner widespread commercial success it was, by no means, the only cryptocurrency or even the first to ever exist. As it happens, multiple digital-cash platforms tried to obtain popularity in a society not even familiar with mobile phones. DigiCash, a company created by David Chaum was the first to gain any positive notoriety—however, innovation before its time tends to plummet—if it cannot be counted on to lay feasible groundwork.

The DigiCash system, which relied on 'blind signatures' did its best to ensure the privacy of any of its users involved in online transactions. As far as safety, the system was fairly foolproof, but businesses were not yet ready to trust something so obscure. As Chaum was unable to find consistent businesses with which his clients could do business, the money had nowhere to go and Chaum was forced to close with less than a decade behind him.

Though still far ahead of its time, pioneers of the system like Chaum and others of the 'Cypherpunk' circle introduced and faced the challenges that held cryptocurrency back in one era— but laid a foundation to be built upon and expanded in the next.

A Changing Legal Climate

Another challenge many of the early pioneers of digital money faced were the legal restrictions imposed. The expanded use of the internet, the connectivity of computers and developments regarding encryption that came to a head in the 1980s spawned the creation of internet money to the wider populace. Before then, the only real use of cryptography was by intelligence and undercover agencies.

With the Internet, however, widespread public and private access to databases and data-mines led to societal change and the need of encryption technology. Laws and information that helped to keep this new frontier safe by implementing encryption tools were the 'Data Encryption Standard' and Dr. Whitefield Diffie's article following the 'Latest Directions of Cryptography'. Finally, Dr. Martin Hellman's work that evolved cryptography in the technological medium and age of the Internet allowed the private sector use through governmental discretion.

Standing on the Shoulders

The creator of Bitcoin, Satoshi Nakamoto, was well aware of the prior legal grounds and foundation set by the pioneers of the industry. Therefore, when he arrived upon the idea of creating a transparent, anonymous, decentralized system, rid of unfortunate double-spending and ensuring its users of privacy and anonymity—he had some semblance of where to begin. And, after trial, error, and a good amount of testing—Nakamoto was able to securely maintain private holdings as users provided an encrypted address kept safe by public and private access keys, and further secured using a sophisticated digital network that allowed both transactions and new coins to be minted through a specified software protocol. In other words, Bitcoin was created.

The Unlikely Pairing

The connection between cryptocurrencies and a clear inspiration for their creation from fiat currency is more than superficial. The relationship between the two is not inherently at odds, either—so far as to say the history of their implementation is remarkably parallel.

For example, in the early years of Bitcoin multiple banking executives of renown came out to denounce cryptocurrency as a fraudulent entity. However, as understanding of the novel system expanded, they backtracked, even so far as outright denying or, at the very least, ignoring prior statements as they began initiatives to use the same technology to expand their own corporate strategies. A centralized system condensing decentralization, so the cards were still held in their favor.

Corporations or large entities in direct control of the technology they propagate has a dangerous precedent in fiat currency.

With a history stretching back to the colonial era and the printing-press, fiat currency developed to generate notes that were given value by the issuance of colonial land.

Fiat Currency vs. Cryptocurrency

In evaluating fiat currencies as they compare to modern-day cryptocurrencies a line can be drawn that connects the framework, and also a projection for cryptocurrency's future. Though reliant on intervention and acceptance from compliant markets, global governance, and relegated control—the future could be found in a study of the past.

As a result of wars with France and India, fiat currencies were developed in the colonial United States to publish money in an effort to pay off debt—a method continued later in its history to rectify the fallout of the Great Depression. The British Parliament had limited oversight or, frankly, concern for colonial debts and so, in an early effort of independence, the colonies created their own terms to deliver on the promises the fiat currencies entailed.

In effect, fiat acted in a way that caused the Royal Government to lose a lot of residual income, as the colonists successfully cut out the middleman. They paid vendors of the Caribbean directly, traded among themselves, and by doing so cut off the Crown's tax revenue on goods. To resolve this measure, Parliament enacted the 'Currency Act of 1754' to cripple this new economic system. And, to the colonist's dismay, it worked. The colonists suffered in their debt, unable to pay it back whether public or private—and, as history teaches, tensions grew.

The Tumultuous History of the Fiat Currency

Drawing a comparison between the growth of fiat currency and cryptocurrency may seem an odd task given the massive technical differences between the two, but there is actually a surprising number of similarities between the stages both monetary systems evolved through.

To begin charting those similarities, it is necessary to dive first into the history and growth of fiat currency in the early modern period.

The late 1600s through the mid-1700's was a period defined by a near constant state of conflict between the expanding colonial powers of France and England. Both nations fought for continental supremacy in Europe for centuries, and with the discovery of the Americas, the scope of that conflict naturally expanded East to involve the fledgling colonial nations still under the rule of distant kings. The most consequential of these wars, the Seven Years' War (also known as the French and Indian War in North America), was concluded with the Royal Decree of 1763. This document saw the French recognize defeat, and allowed the British Crown to subdue those Native American tribes who had sided with the French.

Despite their victory, the British treasury was severely depleted due to the cost of such a global war. To recoup losses and stabilize their economy in Europe, the British launched an extensive campaign to collect debt and taxes from their colonial holdings in North America. The fighting had been brutal and costly in the colonies, as the distance required to move troops and supplies required extensive investments. As a means to meet their new monetary obligations, the colonial government began printing money as a way to pay off the debt.

In the colonial era of North America, there existed three methods of exchange which gave rise to the commodity-based systems, species-based systems, and fiat systems:

In the commodity-based system, colonists would use land staples as a kind of currency for business transactions. This led to a severe imbalance between colonial states, as those that produced products with a higher utility value (such as tobacco, a colonial product highly prized in Europe), had an advantage over states that produced more mundane products.

The species system, in contrast, was a system that used gold and silver as the value item. Due to their nature, species were obviously scarce, which created an issue when buying imports due to the increased flight of assets away from the commodity, depleting the supply.

The limitations on both commodity-based and species-based monetary systems inevitably led to an increase in money printing, and thus the growth of the imperial fiat system.

The fiat practice began in Massachusetts in 1690, and by 1715, ten of the thirteen colonies were printing paper money as a form of currency for payments. This process resulted in a cost-free currency, so long as it was not backed by species. Of course, problems began to emerge quickly with this new system. Hyperinflation and value depreciation began to plague those British merchants and creditors who were paid in the new paper currency.

As resentment in Europe grew to the practice, Parliament was eventually forced to act through the 1751 Currency Act and the later revision of the Act in 1764.

In the early days of the colonial fiat system, the British Parliament had allowed the colonies to construct an alternative financial system to the British pound. This resulted in a roughly 30-year period where the colonial fiat system could act independently, and without oversight from any of the British government's ruling bodies. Left to their own devices, the colonial government did not seek the counsel or advice from the British in governing their new financial system.

In effect, the colonists of North America had used the technologies of ink and the printing-press to create an alternate way of business through paper-notes on credit bills. Colonists could now use this system to subvert taxes, such as the sugar tax, and were able to do business and raise cash fairly independently. This was a possibility due to the colonist's ability to directly pay sellers, a method that bypassed British tax agents.

While the colonial government considered this practice illegal, the colonists were relatively unobstructed, being free to engage in business development and the production of money. In contrast, the loss of revenue was viewed much more seriously by the British government. The Acts imposed by Parliament to counter their tax loss, the Sugar Act of 1764, the Currency Act of 1764, and the Stamp Act of 1765, would have severe consequences for British-Colonial relations, and would eventually be cited as reasons justifying the Revolutionary War.

Given the lack of involvement from either British or colonial governing bodies, it was almost inevitable that a crackdown would occur in the form of legislation and regulation. Eventually, it would come in the form of the Currency Act, instituted against the governments of North America's colonies. The Act worked to abolish the printing of money, making it impossible to use fiat currency or bank bills to pay off private debt. An obvious result of this action was the tightening of money supplies in the colonies, which further encouraged frustration amongst the colonies with the British government's oversight. The Act was heavily contested by colonial governments, who went so far as to send representatives to London who could oppose the act.

This was met with some success, as amendments to the Currency Act were eventually made, that allowed some colonial states such as New York to issue currency in regulated amounts. Finally, during the First Continental Congress, a Bill of Rights was issued that addressed the issues colonists and their governments had with certain acts of Parliament, calling the Currency Act a subversion of their inalienable rights.

Where does that leave Cryptocurrency?

Digital currency is moving fast to impact the global community and has already had a very significant effect on developed countries. In places where the general welfare of large swaths of people are improved, cryptocurrency represents a change in tone as their success story has become a ringing endorsement of the necessity of alternative financial mechanisms. Systems that are employed beyond formal banking using primitive fiat currencies as a means of exchange. In that vein, the new financial path, founded through the innovation of cypherpunks, is on the rise and its exponential reach should be properly analyzed and anticipated by other sectors of society.

A Change to the Status Quo

When it comes down to it, technology can act as a challenger to the government. Whether by the reduction of tax revenue of certain sources, evidenced by the history of the fiat currency and its evolution, or by cultivating an entirely new marketplace—however that doesn't mean the two entities cannot coexist to mutual benefaction. Indeed, government can often align agendas and circumvent lost revenue through engaged study of the newer forms of technology, thereby having a base to institute policy reflective of proposed progress and still protect the public against nefarious uses or threats of technological malpractice. However, that is not the case with banks.

As it stands, technology and, by extension, a push for decentralized cryptocurrency is disruptive to the centralized fiat structure of the banking industry. With that, the primary point of contention arises between the two systems.

While cryptocurrencies are still in their earliest stages, regardless of the long and complicated history of their inception, they have much further to travel before they can compete with the market ranges of traditional banking. Lingering now in the ranges of hundreds of billions for everyday transactions, fiat currencies reside somewhere in the realm of tens of trillions each day. The gap seems to be closing. The public is less wary of this foreign technology and finding themselves comfortable with this new form of currency. In addition, the corrupt entities in some modern banking systems have left the door open for alternative solutions, as the billions unable to participate in the conventional methods are left to wayside—unable to gain economic ground.

Perpetrations of Inequality in the Fiat System

It is surprising how the implementation of a new system allows faults in the old to be seen with a degree of clarity. Not that the faults cannot be mended, but that they have existed for a long time and their drawbacks rooted firmly. In 1790 there were barely four million people residing in the newly formed United States. However, Anglo-Saxon landowners of this new republic were granted the highest benefit of the fiat currency.

Censuses of the type dictate that enslaved peoples made up a little under 14% of the total people. It is also important to note that the census did not count Native Americans which included about six-hundred thousand people across the continent, a steep drop off in population since Columbus' arrival where they were estimated to be about seven million people.

It is important to note these numbers of disregarded peoples as the fiat currency, in its earlier years of existence, ignored nearly 1.3 million people who received little to no support from the system. It is interesting, almost as an economic rendition of the civil debates in the US throughout its history that this new monetary system would begin to give a voice to the voiceless, representation to people who had none—yet still besmirch minorities in the process.

With that in mind, and those arguments on hand, it might be easier to understand why digital coin values, the ideals surrounding inclusion in a predominantly exclusive system, and the further democratization of wealth could resonate with sections of society—predominantly those experiencing financial hardships or otherwise, underbanked.

What is clear, by census numbers and land ownership, is that certain parts of society were excluded from involvement in the fiat systems, whether intended or not, and the number of people outside the benefit realm grew as tensions of inequality until they came to a head with the Civil War and the plausibility of a definitive change.

A Philosophical and Economic Divide

By 1860 the population of the U.S. had grown remarkably to nearly thirty-one million before the onset of the Civil War. And, with that number in mind, the enslaved population accounted for nearly 12% of that number, roughly four million people—perhaps less by percentage but by no means less significant as it represented a monstrously large number of people.

The conclusion of the Civil War and loss of the Confederacy to Abraham Lincoln and his Union troops brought about an apparent end to the horrors of slavery. It was followed by steps toward change and renewed hope to a severely battered country. Lincoln instituted the Freedman Bank, a place designed to alleviate the struggles endured by former slaves, and form a path toward integration, minor restitution, and, overall, a new way forward for the oppressed.

But this institution of this bank was not met without resistance. Indeed, it became a cause of conflict from Lincoln's detractors. Once a symbol of hope and change, congress voted for Freedman Bank's closure not seven years after Lincoln's assassination.

One Step Forward, Two Steps Back

While only a system, the fiat currency and its institutions find themselves capable of exclusion—insulating segments of society and separating the rest by the basic role that banks hold of administering financial services to a prevalent or non-existent consumer base. Banking systems were not officially implemented until the critical congressional decision that arose from the 1863 and 1864 National Banking Acts.

Before those acts, banks were self-regulated by the State's discretion—with very minimal if any federal involvement. With no standardized system implemented, the philosophical divisions of the nation reared themselves in economic forms.

In 1846, the Polk administration started work on a national banking system where public funds were extracted from private banks and then deposited in branches of the treasury. The creation of this national system barely came out of the planning stages before slaves were freed as the conclusion of the Civil War. There was no better time than Post-Civil War and the catastrophe of the Freedman Bank for America to develop a policy of inclusion in the national bank that would provide a monetary system that allowed banks to expand and benefit all segments of society.

The opportunity was not lost on decisionmakers, as the closure of Freedman's and resultant loss of savings among former slaves sowed an intense distrust in the congressional body. All that being said, the National Bank was a step forward for inclusion, but not without an entirely new and twisted history based on a claim of the purported equality of the implementation.

As the fiat system, even the nationwide system implemented in the U.S., endured changes and setbacks that relegated wealth and continued to segment society from an economic standpoint—cryptocurrency has the opportunity to mend these older wounds. While the U.S. might represent a trial-and-error period of the marginalized currency, there is a global elephant in the room as unbanked peoples that are excluded from any exposure to capital, and are denied basic economic services have found themselves trapped beneath the tireless heel of corporate banks.

Not Without Growing Pains

These arguments that frame the fiat system and all its drawbacks come from a well-written and globalized history of capital displacement, from isolation and segmentation of societal groups that have resulted in an outcry for an alternative. Cryptocurrency is not free of its own controversies.

'The Silk Road' was a nefarious marketplace that employed cryptocurrency where criminal dealers of drugs and weapons displayed openly their distribution plans including guns and entire kilo bricks of cocaine. With that in mind, the inherent privacy and anonymity, a major selling point of cryptocurrency emboldened this group suddenly free to deal apart from a central authority. The 'Silk Road' case, in that regard, exposed the problems cryptocurrency critics had warned of, including the ease by which illicit activity could ensue without necessary oversight.

However, in the infancy of its design, cryptocurrency would never be able to operate. Without any regulation, the 'Silk Road' black-market represented a system by which no society could effectively endure. There was no oversight, unfettered criminal activity and a dangerous degree of feeling of invulnerability to law. A convicted founder, Ross Ulbricht, provided a system for illegal activity and no restraint. Drugs, weapons, murder-for-hire, prostitution, laundering, wire fraud, and a litany of other crimes charged in federal court. Although Ulbricht did not commit all these crimes personally, he allowed the conduit for which they could be committed. In that regard, he was sentenced to two life-terms without parole. All that being said, his creation of a technology that used Bitcoin as a currency of exchange allowed government officials, prosecutors and detractors to send a warning, using Ulbricht as a poster-child, of the consequence of unregulated black-markets that instituted cryptocurrency.

A Warning Instituted

As it goes, longstanding prison sentences are usually enough to dissuade future movements. However, the case of the 'Silk Road' and Ulbricht cast a dark shadow over cryptocurrencies to some. Conversely, it also served as a new means to innovate, to make the system safer by adding to the revolutionary blockchain technology features of smart contracts.

In years since, the dark shadow cast by the 'Silk Road' have nearly dissipated as the criminality has been dissuaded by advancements in the technology. With the help of financiers and lawyers, along with a collaboration of technologists and governing entities—there has spawned a foundational frame to prosecute violators of cryptocurrency. With implementations of advisory positions that assist crypto upcomers designing their core business around the technology, a safer version of the currency exists that has and continues to gain traction in the cultural and retail communities. Not to mention, cryptocurrency has evolved near exponentially in the investment realm as the hedge fund strategists look to Bitcoin's price variance to enact decisions.

Inherent Value and Technological Minimalism

Another point of overlap between the fiat and crypto currency systems comes from the dissolution of value-based commodities. Gold and silver are metals with inherent value in our economic system and that age-old methodology overlapped as the fiat system embraced it. However, just as we moved from the necessity of carrying large quantities of tangible gold and silver, so too have we removed the inherent value of them for economic use. From a purely common-sense approach, people wanted less actual currency on them to avoid loss in case of robbery. The transference of metals to dollars, from inherent value to perceived value has gone a step further still—as we moved in the fiat system to something less physical. However, many parts of the fiat system are still represented by physical means, especially to the unbanked that must store accrued wealth by other means. With that in mind, robberies to the unbanked can be more economically damaging as they are in possession of wealth, not representations of wealth.

Consequently, the unbanked see even more reason to turn to the safety of cryptocurrencies to ensure that profit accrued can be kept and wealth cultivated, even without the need for a modern banking system. Examination of the reasons for cryptocurrency use relegates themselves to three primary points: the use of money to make money, equitable value in trade, and an effective, agreed upon means of exchange.

Use Money to Make Money

One of the hardest things to come to terms with digital currency is its commercial appeal and the professionally qualified requirements to trade effectively. Just as the stock market, it can be dangerous for some individuals to get swept up in the excitement of the crypto surge over the past few years like the rising price per shar of Bitcoin, Litecoin, or Ethereum— and spend money they don't have on poor investment decisions. There are small scale investments in cryptocurrency where people can dip their toes in the water, so to speak, and see how they fare. With hundreds of currencies presently available on marketplaces like Coinbase that can be used as an investment manager, there is opportunity to be sure. However, the standard rules of stock investment still apply as 'pump and dump' methodologies or 'FOMO' practices could negatively impact personal wealth.

Equitable Value

Tokens in cryptocurrency as a derivative of blockchain implementation decreases the volatility of the trade floor but still doesn't make it entirely stable. The familiarity of inherent value allows for prospective users, through mobile devices or otherwise, to safely explore the new frontier without anything more substantial as risk than the medium of regular transaction payments. The ICOs integrated through blockchain data provide an effect method of trade value and value storage. However, the continued exploration of blockchain points toward models that may coincide with the decreasing volatility of investments making the jumps less extreme.

Agreed Upon Means of Exchange

The only way to truly grow cryptocurrency, however, is with the acceptance of it from a governmental level—a measure that accepts it as an alternative and viable currency. It cannot happen without first understanding the potential effects of the currency.

While the government regulators are ardently developing legal machinations to handle technologies that are found to be disruptive to people's health—polices enacted involve procedures set around MSBs to stifle money laundering and any other form of fraud. However, agencies could still do more by holding workshops and employing crypto-consultants to create internal data-banks on the subject—training and designing and effective framework that doesn't hinder innovation, but offers a structure by which governing bodies can protect against the harms aforementioned in the 'Silk Road.'

The upgrade of government talent-pools surrounding the banking industry, as well as hiring resources experienced in the underlying technological machinations of cryptocurrency are another good start. To effect, the Bermuda Island is a proper illustration of just how a legislation can be enacted that serves to implement a cryptocurrency business. Bermuda has put in place a fair, yet equally strict system of AML (anti-money laundering) and other enforcement to dissuade any illicit trade activities. Thusly, their established legal framework works to modernize and hasten the ICO process, creating somewhat of a 'gold-standard' in domiciled ICOs.

To be sure, governments play perhaps the most pivotal role in managing the agreement between both centralized and decentralized payment networks. To completely push for the erasure of the banking system isn't plausible. Centralized banks still have a role to play in a society's economic stature, as well as their well-being. However, that doesn't negate new software like cryptocurrency from creating an option that might be a more plausible choice of exchange when centralized banking is no longer a feasible reality.

The important thing to understand is less how these two forms of currency are different, but how one is understood and the other still, even years later, seems obscure. As government's work to understand digital currencies, they might see how they can work a complimentary practice of formal fiat systems. With the implementation of compliant systems that work together, innovation could endure while the safety of the consumer is never compromised and corruption of certain systems, whether fraudulent or isolating, are never accepted outright.

Acceptance of Cryptocurrency as a Tradeable Asset

In 2017, cryptocurrency trading entered the mainstream market and took it for a ride. Bitcoin's return on investment of nearly 1300% was monumental, and marked one of the best returns of all time. And, just as the value has only increased in the years that followed, so too has interest. Google searches for 'Bitcoin' and 'cryptocurrency' have risen just as media outlets covering the surge. It wasn't a wonder when blockchain investments doubled by the end of 2017, exceeding twenty million by the year's end. Additionally, as tokens have become an invaluable asset, businesses accepting the virtual money have increased in conjunction.

This change carried over into 2018, as somewhere around two-hundred thousand commercial transactions occurred daily. The astounding growth in a year's time was noteworthy, but when compared to the millions of an entity like Visa, they barely made a dent. And as time wore on, the specific characteristics of cryptocurrency were made known. To expand, the volatile nature of the currency influences how well it stores value, which consequently limits its exchange use. Put simply, if someone buys Bitcoin at a fixed value, and Bitcoin's value drops, they lose money.

Volatile by Nature

The up-and-down nature of cryptocurrency returns of 2017 show constant fluctuation, but overall upward trends. Bitcoin valuation increased thirteen times, while other cryptocurrencies like Ripple saw a 36,000% increase. However, the volatility on a daily basis means acceptance of cryptocurrency was less open-armed.

Although, this has ultimately played to crypto's benefit—as it made more interested parties speculative, and mainstream audiences open. To that effect, over the last years, purchasing crypto has become more widespread, and far easier. Though still volatile, it's garnered viral acclaim. The increase in popularity allowed tons of exchange traded funds (ETFs) which offered investors a chance to bring exposure to newer currencies. Meanwhile, other ETFs cover the underlying companies that offer blockchain services—as more established exchanges like the Chicago Mercantile Exchange (CME) can still embrace the new market. All said, there is no shortage of ways to invest in rising or established cryptocurrencies.

Determining Value

Dedicated valuation is a hugely important aspect of investment. Additionally, the creation of liquid financial markets goes a long way to establish value. As a comparison, stock markets are tasked with price discovery, or an agreed upon clearing price. As more buyers and sellers enter the market, the market becomes 'liquid'. A more liquid market leads to better price discovery, and dominoes down to higher trade volumes. Also, in effect, stability.

All that said, despite the influx in buyers and sellers, the crypto market is anything but efficient. Unable to sway its price volatility makes it indicative of a challenge in establishing base value. The rise and fall of Bitcoin, in large share volumes, makes for a speculative market. However, due to the novel nature of the currency, it's also possible that typical measures are not apt to be applied.

Bitcoin is a prime example—first created to be a borderless virtual currency, strategists measure with metrics that rely on positioning, inflation, and a country's exchange rates. However, none of those parameters apply to a global currency. All that said, the best way it seems to determine valuation is from comparison. Ethereum and the smart contact groups of blockchain has created even more interest, in some respects, than Bitcoin. However, both residing as established cryptocurrencies, their values have moved similarly. Therefore, it could be noted that perception of asset class is as good a measure as any for valuation.

A Short History of Development for Cryptocurrencies

In terms of age for cryptocurrency, its barely out of infancy. However, in the short time, and expansive rate of technological growth working in conjunction, it has seen some amazing steps forward. From 10,000 Bitcoins equating to a $25 pizza order in 2010 to $41,000 a coin—it's safe to say it's grown rather exponentially.

With a market capitalization sitting at around $780 billion flowing up and down from its 2017 burst, continued advances in the technology keep cryptocurrency markets on the upward trend. All that in mind, this short list covers moments of importance in the development of our modern-day cryptocurrencies and news related to their fluctuating valuations:

June 2011:

- Gawker article shines a light on Bitcoin's role in the 'Silk Road'.

- Burst of interest to crypto as means of exchange, even for illicit practices.

- Value rises after the widespread article distribution nearly 80%.

March 2013:

- Software update incompatible with parts of BTC network caused structural reformat.

- Multiple mining firms agreed to forgo mined coins to facilitate downgrade, which had no immediate impact on prices. BTC 's price increased by 40%.

- Cyprus financial crisis and banking system's imminent collapse required a rescue that taxed high-valued banks.

- Bitcoin's bailout and ability to work outside laws and centralized banks is recognized by the financial world causing its value to double a week after the bailout.

October 2013:

- Silk Road is shut down.

- Owner and operator Ross Ulbricht arrested on charges of money laundering, computer hacking, and drug trafficking.

- FBI seized 144,000 Bitcoins as part of the arrest, which was subsequently sold in different blocks in 2014 and

2015, netting $48 million.

- Bitcoin's value shuddered briefly.

November 2013:

- U.S. Senate and People's Bank of China provide legitimacy to cryptocurrencies by failing to declare them as an enemy of the state.

- Hearings recognize the technology's innovative nature, while PBOC's then deputy governor offered widespread investment in Bitcoin market.

- Exchange became regulated, limitations placed on the country's currency.

- Renminbi, China surged in Bitcoin interest, raising value.

December 2013:

- PBOC declares that Bitcoin is not a currency and prohibits financial institutions from conducting business with the cryptocurrency.

- Year nearly concluded with Bitcoin value at $1,130, but value falls to just over $500 in the week following the announcement.

February 2014:

- Challenging year to start as Bitcoin endures several hacks or external attacks.

- Mt. Gox became extensively vulnerable, a successful hack costing it nearly 1 million coins.

- Mt. Gox filed for bankruptcy toward the end of the month.

- Bitcoin's value dropped once more, nearly 50% to a $450 low by month's end.

August 2016:

- Bitfinex, newly minted as the highest price cryptocurrency exchange, is hacked for $120,000.

- Bitcoin's price is relatively stable after the hack, but value fell by 15% in the days that preceded press-release, increasing worry about the threat of insider information dealing.

April 2017:

- Japan becomes the first country to recognize Bitcoin as a legal currency.

- Japan moves to forefront of the cryptocurrency debate as Mt. Gox is located in Tokyo.

- Although Bitcoin is recognized as a legal payment-method, still not regarded as legal tender.

- Cryptocurrency confusion for holders in Japan, where currency is treated more like an asset than real merchandise.

- Bitcoin burgeoned in 2017, rising almost 30% in April to an all-time high of $2,400.

September 2017:

- China shows pushback on cryptocurrencies unregulated features.

- All ICOs in the country are barred in early September, followed promptly by a shut-down of all cryptocurrency exchanges toward the end of the month.

- Questions flutter among the mining community within the country as they feared targeting by government (eventual to occur in 2018)

- With a negative market impact, Bitcoin fell 30% during the first half of the month

- Press releases in contradiction caused influx to allow recovery of 70% by month's end.

October to December 2017:

- Chicago Mercantile Exchange (CME) and Chicago Options Exchange Board (COEB) announce and offer the first Bitcoin futures contracts, with U.S. approval.

- Commission on Commodity Futures Trading instituted.

- New market entrants subsequently rise as Coinbase reports 100,000 new users following the CME announcement.

- Prices grow from November to December, as Ethereum increases five times their worth and Bitcoin increases three times theirs.

May/June 2018:

- Market manipulation problems occur as the U.S. Department of Justice (DOJ) initiate a criminal probe to conclude whether or not traders used nefarious tactics (spoofing or flooding) to influence prices.

- A University of Texas paper is published by Professor John Griffin and Amin Shams that argues the credibility of price manipulation as a culprit or even responsible for rising cryptocurrency values in half of reported figures from 2017.

- Valuations weaken throughout the year, with Bitcoin falling 30% in May and June.

- Coinrail, a Korean based cryptocurrency exchange, is hacked for a value of $40 million. Neither Bitcoin or Ethereum currencies were stolen.

- Event added to the negative impression on the market

- Both cryptocurrencies fell in the news by more than 10%.

July 2019:

- Bitcoin spikes in value as Facebook and other organizations launch their own forms of cryptocurrency and flood the market.

- Facebook announces 'Libra' for 2020, independent crypto supported by member companies.

March 2020:

- Cryptocurrency Act of 2020 offered legislative oversight
  to less regulated forms of cryptocurrency in the world
  affected by pandemic.

Reflection on a Tumultuous Past

The past several years saw meteoric rises and compounding
falls of cryptocurrency. To add, there has also been no shortage
of negative and positive news surrounding the impact and
development of their trading. While patterns exist in the volatile
nature of the endeavor, traders and investors further interest
show a more widespread acceptance of the technology. Clearly,
the entire system has experienced a multitude of growing pains,
but it has also excelled at a rate almost incomparable.

Following a decline in 2018 after the monumental rise of
Bitcoin in 2017, cryptocurrency has continued its upward trend
even reaching an all-time high at the conclusion of 2020 and the
ill-effects of the worldwide pandemic.

As many hopeful investors cling to the possibility for rapid
growth, the crypto market seems to be experiencing a relative
point of calm. As some of the most critical points in
cryptocurrencies history revolve around the implementation of
Bitcoin as a widely accepted exchange medium, whether
through illicit or legal means—it still goes to show how
marketability is directly tied to growth. Even infamy, in that
regard, garners interest. However, during the banking crisis of
Cyprus, Bitcoin truly showed the value in its borderless, indeed
nearly boundless nature. It's offering as an alternative to the
clear and present dangers of centralized banking were nothing

short of a miracle.

All that said, as the volatility of share price continues to be up-and-down while steadily rising, the interest in frequent trading doesn't lend much hope for a stabilized market in the traditional sense. It also brings about the need for more regulated scrutiny as separate markets expand. Although investors should be aware of the change, it also encourages that academics are needed to fundamentally discern and perhaps evolve how cryptocurrencies are measured—as traditional means still seem inadequate.

Traditional Markets vs. ICOs

Investing in cryptocurrency has gone through certain evolutions as well. While ICOs in crypto are most similarly regarded to IPOs in the stock-market, they do still draw comparisons to venture capital (VC) and crowd-sourced efforts. To start, IPOs are often needed to raise money or allow owners to make money from their new investment. The process of an IPO usually means a business has been around the block long enough that investors can determine its value ahead of time. That said, IPOs are uncommon for start-ups or young businesses, as their valuations are less documented. While it isn't completely implausible, a company using an IPO should have some years behind them, if not decades. An IPO that experiences some degree of success is able to get investors pumped up about the potential of the investment from longstanding valuations and projections. With that in mind, registered brokers handle the sales, and there are strictly laid out rules to what can occur during the stages of that sale. For example, the SEC finds themselves involved and nothing can go forward without a statement of their say-so.

To that end, underwriters can proceed to take orders, and as a by-product of the action, help make a determination of the stock. However, it is important to note that SEC doesn't have jurisdiction overseas, and only covers those listed on the U.S. exchange. This results in companies listing their stocks in multiple markets to increase the shareholder base and equity potential.

Beyond the public nature of IPOs, venture capital is a private investment—one that typically occurs from within but that isn't always the case. That said, the money usually comes from outside sources, or even close personal sources, to fund the infancy of certain operations. However, different pools of capital within venture capital investments vary. Some reflect start-ups, while others try to help businesses evolve to maintain their creditability in a changing market. In that vein, 'angel investors' are often those early investors. They take on the high-risk of fallout, or a business not getting off the ground, which plays homage to their name. That said, it isn't without their tricks as the angel investor usually invests for a large cut of the pie.

Last to mention are crowd-sourced efforts. Yet another method by which venture funding can offer help to start-ups, this ranges from one wealthy investor to multiple, making it a somewhat democratic process. That said, the broad group does not usually have as much say-so in the direction of the company as an angel investor might—they appreciate the goal and see its potential without much in-depth input. With that in mind, the risk associated is typically far less than more direct forms of venture capital approaches, and as a result there is less overwatch from hopeful investors waiting anxiously to turn a profit whether by encouraging a merger or other means.

Before moving on, while there is a certain appeal to crowd-sourced funding and maintaining a sort of creative control over business endeavors, streamlined venture capitalist investors usually come with multiple tools in their arsenal to make the most of the business, not to mention relationships built over time. They are professionals at evaluating early-stage businesses and further at setting early valuations. They know where a business has the potential to go and what steps should be taken to get it there.

The Difference in ICOs

Based on those alternative sources, ICOs have a good bit in common. At the early stages, they share similar risks of VC investment but also the freedom of an IPO. Once on the crypto-exchange, they are free to be traded after launching. That said, successful ICOs are still vetted as heavily to ensure the prospective success and work out problems ahead of time. A successful ICO always needs a good starting point, passionate idea, well-documented white paper, adorned by proper management and talented tech team—another boon is garnered interest by the still closely knit community.

However, for all the comparisons, ICOs are still a fairly unique method and gaining traction. As their potential is evaluated more investors seem to be jumping on board. But since there doesn't seem to be any lack of ICO hopefuls, standing out in an increasingly saturated marketplace can be difficult. That said, the potential of these blockchain-inspired applications, created within the bounds of a community ready for something new and offering a multitude of crowd-sourced options—start-up and evolving ICOs seem to have no intention of slowing down.

Variants on Trading Cryptocurrencies

The good news about joining the market this year, is that it's never been easier to do so. With a wild influx in popularity, buying and trading virtual currency is a breeze. Apps like Coinbase allow users to link their centralized bank accounts and push them to the limits of decentralized commodities. Because, just as there was a boom in the number of cryptocurrencies available over the last decade, so too have increased their number of trading arenas. However, as only Mt. Gox existed in the earlier days, highlights the risk of crypto working against its intended means by existing at all in a centralized location—the reputation of the endeavor and technology has since been mended. In the past years, global exchanges have seen a multifold increase bringing crypto to the mainstream with larger investments in a huge way.

Variants on Trading Crypto-Assets

There is some exhaustive legislative red-tape that is often taken for granted in the traditional investment marketplace. However, those same procedures and inherent protections cannot be thrown aside with cryptocurrency. That said, it's best to treat crypto as a stock market.

When you trade on the crypto market, you are fluctuating parties at a greater means than other investments. It's almost as if taking sides, moving soldiers from one camp to another. Without efficient trade linkages often attributed to the traditional stock market, crypto lacks the ability to create an arbitrage opportunity. The point where you can purchase stocks at a cheaper rate and sell for significantly more. This arbitrage closes gaps quickly, as the price differences for the same asset vanish. Conversely, in a crypto market, the market prices for the same assets could vary by a few percentage points at least. Differences are more greatly attributed to varying exchange liquidity, than any traditional stock-based arbitrage means.

With all that in mind, investors should walk in with the impression imprinted that all the exchanges have moderate regulation, and the decision of the right domicile is extremely important. That said, while the bigger exchanges are limited in flexibility, some smaller exchanges offer down rates, innovations in pricing, and ultimately more opportunity to trade. However, as this digital marketplace offers openings to technologically savvy individuals, hacking is still a concern.

Exchange Problems Still Posed

The other issue to consider as cryptocurrency works to emerge from its infancy, is a lack of exchange in foreign fiat markets. That said, although it seems almost abhorrent to suggest cashing out your well-earned crypto trades in paper-money—not many businesses, debt collectors, or landlords will allow the use of cryptocurrency for payment substitute. As it goes, the simple transference of crypto gains to fiat currency are a strange necessity. However, if your gains exist in a foreign country, though the crypto is borderless, the transaction with a country involved might prove challenging.

Further, something similar appears when creating various accounts on various apps, as each transaction might entail their own funding requirements. For example, Coinbase will let users attach credit cards, but a lot of other exchanges will not. Bitfinex, to that end, only allows coin deposits. The important thing to note, in that regard, is choosing crypto exchanges that feature the currencies you desire a more jurisdictional questions are handled case by case. As most all exchanges feature the big names like Bitcoin, some newer start-ups will not be featured. That isn't to say one day they won't be, but it takes a certain degree of notoriety and, as with the market as a whole, more involvement in trading. As hundreds are added each quarter, there is no shortage of options.

Preventative Security Measures

All that said, after a number of hacks that have negatively and detrimentally impacted multiple exchanges globally, increase in crypto security is a clear reactive and now, proactive, measure. As Mt. Gox, though one of the largest exchanges early on, was still driven to bankruptcy from attacks. Another big attack that happened on Coincheck in 2018 lost the exchange $500 million in coins. The difference in years made the influx of crypto much more popular and thus the loss much more palpable, but those are the larger cases. A multitude of smaller hacks have also occurred which resulted in dozens of smaller exchanges closing and would-be investors backing out. As there is yet to be SIPC insurance for cryptocurrency exchanges, finding a company among the many that hold assets offline is a diamond in the rough. However, that means of protection is extremely important and among the first steps of preventative security as a majority of hacks occurred with coin depositories or Internet bound hot-wallets. If investors have the ability to take their coins offline and store them safely in a storage device—they can worry less about the always online dangers. Though, safety with a bit of irony as then the coins are somewhat centralized and vulnerable on your person.

Variant and Volatile Trends of Cryptocurrency

There is no shortage of popular trends present in the crypto world—one such being the ICO. While still speculative in certain countries, subject to heavy-handed oversight, data carries that only a few ICOs were able to reach their first anniversary. Indeed, by the end of 2017 nearly half had floated and the portion raised was somewhere near $500 billion. Another cautionary tale came from the sheer amount of ICO scams. As they were offered under different names, levels of in-depth disclosures, some even appeared as a crowd-sourced fundraiser. While many of the scams were shut-down with no much drawback, it does little to ease those that did suffer losses.

That said, all sorts of scams have reared their heads including attempts at a crypto-Ponzi-scheme like iFan and Pincon, that attempted to collect millions from thousands before folding in on themselves. To rectify that situation, Vietnam offices claimed offices outside its borders as far as Dubai—lending credence to the unfortunate consequence of everything loved about crypto: it's borderless and scantly regulated existence.

A Continued Evolution

Perhaps the most important thing to note is that cryptocurrency is not static. If the 'Silk Road' and early instances of cryptocurrencies history could be taken as anything, they should be taken as a warning of the completely unregulated experience of cryptocurrency—and how a society, much like an economy, cannot function in that kind of market.

As digital currencies continue to grow, cultivating their own marketplaces of user interaction—so too will their methods of implementation and the sophistication of their systems.

CHAPTER ELEVEN

BIRTH OF ETHEREUM AND SMART CONTRACTS

Ethereum is the second-largest cryptocurrency by market capitalization, only behind Bitcoin. It is a decentralized open-source blockchain based platform with smart contract functionalities. Ether is the cryptocurrency that Ethereum miners generate as a reward for computations that are performed to secure the blockchain. As of May 2020, Ethereum has served as the platform for more than 260,000 different cryptocurrencies, including 4 of the top 10 by market capitalization cryptocurrencies: EOS, Tether, Binance Coin and Ethereum itself.

Ethereum provides the Ethereum Virtual Machine (EVM),

a decentralized virtual machine that can execute scripts using an international network of public nodes. Contrary to others like Bitcoin Script, the instruction set for the virtual machine is Turing-complete. "Gas," a pricing mechanism for internal transactions, is used to mitigate spam and allocate resources on the network.

In late 2013, Ethereum was proposed by Vitalik Buterin, a cryptocurrency researcher and programmer. Development was funded by an online crowd sale running from July to August 2014. Then, on 30 July 2015, the system went live, with 72 million coins minted. This contains nearly 65% of the total supply circulating in April 2020.

Ethereum, in 2016, was divided into two distinct blockchains following the exploitation of a weakness in the DAO project's smart contract software, and subsequent theft of $50 million worth of ether. With the theft reversed, the new separate version became Ethereum (ETH), and the original chain continued as Ethereum Classic (ETC).

Understanding Ether

"Ether is the digital token (or cryptocurrency) associated with the blockchain Ethereum. In other words, the Coin is Ether, and the Platform is Ethereum" (Chris Hoffman 2018). However, those terms are often used interchangeably by people now. Coinbase, for example, helps you to purchase Ethereum tokens — that is, Ether tokens.

Ethereum tokens are generally categorized as an "altcoin," which really only means a cryptocurrency, which is not Bitcoin. Like Bitcoin, Ethereum is operated on a mostly decentralized network — in this case, the Ethereum blockchain.

Developers wishing to build applications or "smart contracts" on the Ethereum blockchain, need the Ether token to pay for hosting nodes while users of Ethereum-based apps may need Ether to pay for services in those devices. People could also offer services outside the Ethereum network and allow payment in Ether, or exchange Ether tokens for cash – much like Bitcoin.

THE BIRTH OF ETHEREUM

In a white paper late 2013, Vitalik Buterin, a programmer and co-founder of Bitcoin Magazine, initially established Ethereum intending to create decentralized apps. Buterin had claimed that Bitcoin needed to develop applications using a scripting language. He suggested the creation of a new platform with a more general language for scripting, in the absence of agreement.

Ethereum was unveiled at the North American Bitcoin Conference held in Miami in January 2014. Ethereum has an incredibly long list of founders. Anthony Di Iorio wrote, "Ethereum was founded in December 2013 by Vitalik Buterin, Myself, Charles Hoskinson, Mihai Alisie, & Amir Chetrit (initial 5). Joseph Lubin, Gavin Wood, & Jeffrey Wilke were added as founders in early 2014." Early 2014 a Swiss company, Ethereum Switzerland GmbH (EthSuisse), began the formal development of the Ethereum software project. Before the software could be implemented, the basic idea of putting executable smart contracts in the blockchain needed to be specified; this work was done by Gavin Wood, then chief technology officer, in the Ethereum Yellow Paper specifying the Ethereum Virtual Machine. After that, a Swiss non-profit foundation, the Ethereum Foundation (Stiftung Ethereum), was also created. Development was funded during July – August 2014 through an online public crowd sale, with participants buying the Ethereum value token (ether) with another digital currency, Bitcoin.

In March 2017, the creation of the Enterprise Ethereum Alliance (EEA) with 30 founding members was announced by various blockchain start-ups, research groups, and Fortune 500 companies. By May, there were 116 members of the non-profit organization — including ConsenSys, CME Group, Cornell University Research Group, Merck KGaA, Canada National Bank, Samsung SDS, Cooley LLP, J.P. Morgan, Toyota Research Institute, BNY Mellon, Deloitte, Accenture, Banco Santander, Intel, ING, DTCC, and Microsoft. By July 2017, the alliance had more than 150 members, including recent additions from MasterCard, Cisco Systems, Sberbank, and Scotiabank.

The Ethereum Foundation developed several codenamed prototypes of the Ethereum platform prior to the official launch of the Frontier network as part of their Proof-of-Concept show. In July 2015, "Frontier" marked the tentative release of the Ethereum platform by experiment.

WHAT ARE SMART CONTRACTS?

Smart contracts are virtual machine applications running on Ethereum. This is a decentralized "world computer" where all of the Ethereum nodes provide the computing power to run applications. Any nodes that offer computing power for the operation of the Ethereum platform are paid for that resource using Ether tokens.

The contracts written on Ethereum are called smart contracts because when the requirements are met, you can write "contracts" that are automatically executed.

Imagine, for example, building a crowdfunding service like Kickstarter on top of Ethereum. Somebody could set up a smart Ethereum contract, which would pool money for someone else to be sent. The smart contract should be written to tell the receiver everything will be sent when $100,000 in currency is added to the pool. Or, if the threshold of $100,000 has not been met within a month, then all money will be returned to the currency's original holders. This would, of course, use Ether tokens, instead of US dollars.

All this would happen according to the smart contract code, which executes the transactions automatically without a trusted third party needing to hold the money and sign off on the transaction. For instance, on a $100,000 crowdfunding project, Kickstarter takes a 5% charge in addition to a 3% to 5% payment processing cost, which will imply $8000 to $10000 in fees. A smart contract would not require a third party, such as Kickstarter, to pay the fees.

One can use smart contracts for many different things. Developers may build smart contracts that offer certain smart contracts features, similar to how software libraries operate. Or smart contracts may be used as an app to store information about the Ethereum blockchain.

Someone must send sufficient Ether as a transaction fee to execute smart contract code – how much of it depends on the computing resources required. This pays for the participation and the provision of their computing power to the ethereum nodes.

One of the most well-known applications built on the Ethereum network using smart contracts is CryptoKitties.

CryptoKitties are a form of digital "collectible" that is held on the Ethereum blockchain. CryptoKitties provides a good demonstration of how digital items can be stored and exchanged on the Ethereum network.

New CryptoKitties are generated by "breeding," that involves the choosing of two CryptoKitties base and the spending of Ether tokens to run a smart contract. The contracts spawn a new CryptoKitty with the two chosen cats. These kitties and the breeding process details are stored on the public ledger of the Ethereum blockchain.

CryptoKitties that are stored on the Ethereum blockchain ledger can be owned. You can sell them to others or trade them or buy them. This is different from using a mobile app where cats can be purchased, exchanged, and raised. This will usually be stored on the servers of the app itself, and if the company shuts down the app or banned your account, you could lose your precious digital pets. But this cannot happen because CryptoKitties are held on the blockchain. No one can take away your kitties.

In December 2017, coincidentally, when Bitcoin experienced it's all-time high price — people had spent $12 Million equivalent of Ether tokens on CryptoKitties, and CryptoKitty's most expensive digital cat was sold for about

$120,000. CryptoKitties, like Ether, Bitcoin, and costly paintings, are worth anything consumers are prepared to pay.

THE BIRTH OF SMART CONTRACTS

Computer scientist, lawyer, and cryptographer Nick Szabo, who coined the term, initially proposed smart contracts in early 1994. In 1998, the term was used to describe objects that were part of the Stanford Digital Library Project in the rights management service layer of the system The Stanford Infobus.

Since the 2015 release of Ethereum, "smart contract" is also defined more specifically in the sense of computing for specific purposes that occur on a blockchain or distributed ledger. In this interpretation, used by the Ethereum Foundation or IBM, for example, a smart contract is not necessarily related to the traditional idea of a contract; it may be some form of a computer program. A smart contract can also be regarded as a secured stored procedure since its execution and codified effects such as the transfer of some value between parties are strictly enforced and cannot be manipulated after a transaction with specific contract details is stored in a blockchain or distributed ledger. That's because the platform controls and audits the actual execution of contracts and not the arbitrary server-side programs that connect to the platform.

By implementing the Decree on Digital Economic Development in 2017, Belarus became the first country ever to legalize smart contracts. Belarusian lawyer Denis Aleinikov is classified as the author of the legal concept of a smart contract introduced by the decree.

A report from the US Senate in 2018 said: While smart

contracts may sound new, the concept is rooted in fundamental contract law. The judicial system usually adjudicates contractual disputes and enforces terms, but it is also common to have another method of arbitration, especially for international transactions. With smart contracts, the contract built into the code is enforced by a program.

CHAPTER TWELVE

THE GREAT ALTCOIN BUBBLE OF 2017

Factors that affect the price of Altcoins

" **A**n investor will agree to invest in oil if they think the world is running out of oil supply while demand for it remains consistent, or even increases. Similarly, investors in digital currency will only be interested in altcoins that have the potential to add some form of benefit or utility to the lives of people, thereby creating significant demand for the altcoin which has limited supply of its token in market.

The second significant factor is price. Stock investors will look at Apple's $300-plus share price tag along with a north valuation of $1 trillion and deem it overly expensive. In the cryptocurrency space, the same holds true as investors prefer undervalued and "hidden-gem" opportunities rather than bloated and overvalued assets.

A good altcoin has to meet both conditions. A concept that benefits numerous people but is too expensive is of little interest to cryptocurrency investors who are mostly speculators. A cheap but useless altcoin that offers users zero benefits will fade into irrelevance very quickly. Investors are wise to look for altcoins that check off both criteria.

Over 2,000 cryptocurrencies are traded on various digital currency exchanges in some form. The trading of these assets is no different from commodities or stocks. A cryptocurrency exchange brings buyers and sellers together to facilitate transactions between those who wish to purchase a coin and those who want to sell their coin.

For more than one reason, 2017 was a record year for cryptocurrencies. Bitcoin blew up. For the first time, ICO mania set in, and certain altcoins made gains of over 36,000%; the general public for the first time became pretty much aware of cryptocurrencies and took effort to participate in it even if it was driven by greed and fear of missing out (FOMO).

Cryptocurrencies, to say the least, had an incredible run in 2017. One major factor which has altered is back when Bitcoin was $960 per coin in 2016, its market capitalization at the time dominated all 1,300 altcoins by 90%. It was the first cryptocurrency with a market value of more than a billion dollars. On December 25, 2016, it had a market capitalization of approximately $14 billion.

THE RISE OF THE ALTCOIN

As successful as Bitcoin was in raising its valuation in 2017, the altcoin market cap as a whole rose from $2.2 billion at the start of 2017 to over $350 billion.

Currencies such as Monero, Ripple, Dash, NEM, and Ethereum multiplied by as much as 100-fold (or more) in value throughout the year of 2017. Additionally, some altcoins gained legitimacy from financial institutions.

For example, financial institutions around the world embraced the Ripple technology as a means of transferring value; Dash was integrated into hundreds (and growing) of online stores as a means of payment.

There are now thousands of altcoins in existence, and new ones are being created each day. The market cap on cryptocurrency as a whole may surpass trillion dollars soon.

THE ALTCOIN BUBLE

2017 was the year of digital currencies. Bitcoin started the year at $993/BTC and ended at more than $13,000/BTC, a gain of 1,200%. Other notable ones, such as Ethereum and Litecoin, saw similar gains. Yet the rise of altcoins and ICOs in 2017 was even more impressive. While Bitcoin rose by 1,000% over the entire year, alternative cryptocurrencies such as Ripple (XRP) increased by 1,000% over the month of December 2017 alone.

Other smaller cryptocurrencies experienced similar increases. On the back of good marketing, these quick growers often gain significant market capitalization. Individual investors hear of a rising project and don't want to miss out on the opportunity to invest. This fear of missing out loop fueled investment frenzy, leaving even the creators of an ICO or altcoin occasionally puzzled by the rising coin price.

A lot of investors noticed similarities between the current cryptocurrency landscape and the 2000 dot com bubble. Back in 1998-2000, online firms on the stock exchange were massively overvalued. Investment poured into any company that claims to be internet-based, even though the company didn't show any real inherent value or innovative ideas. Many traditional companies attached ".com" to their titles in those days, which saw increased investment immediately.

The same goes for today. Companies add their names to "blockchain" and attract investment. Manufacturers of Iced Tea and bovine breeding firms have modified their labels to be blockchain-friendly, both with significant results. Besides traditional companies changing their names, all you need to do with an ICO to make millions of dollars is apparently a flashy website and a white paper. Forbes estimates that in 2017, ICO's raised $5 billion.

There is a very common investment axiom which goes as, "Don't invest in things don't make sense." In 2017, it was common occurrence to see team of few people writing an ICO whitepaper listing two reasons to invest in their project with a fancy website and being able to successfully raise millions of dollars for projects. That just doesn't make sense. It's during those occasions that one needs to question the market whether the market is in bubble territory because of FOMO or not?

The period of 2017 looked a lot like the Internet Dot Com

bubble of 1999-2000.

TOP ALTCOINS PERFORMANCE OF 2017 BASED ON FORTUNE JACK ANALYSIS

2017 was a landmark year for cryptocurrencies. You could go on a train ride and the chances of you hearing people having conversation about Bitcoin, Ethereum and which altcoin to buy to get their Lamborghinis fast would be high. The technical and subject matter experts in Blockchain and Digital Currencies invested their money soundly while retail investors invested in cryptocurrencies, at the time, like they were gambling. Even gambling websites offered derivatives and advice on cryptocurrencies in 2017 as it became akin to sports and recreational gambling. According to casino and Bitcoin gambling site Fortune Jack (Fintech Futures 2018), following were the top altcoins in 2017 based purely on price growth and market cap:

Ethereum

Ethereum overtook Bitcoin in 2017 in terms of ROI, which increased by 9,162% compared to 1,000% of Bitcoin when the bull run of 2017 started.

Ripple

Ripple made remarkable progress in 2017 with the highest growth compared to all of the major digital currencies – an unbelievable 36,018% increase in 2017. And by market cap, Ripple overtook Ethereum in December for the number two spot.

Litecoin

Launched in 2011 by a retired Google engineer, Litecoin is known as the silver to the gold in bitcoin, with the market cap reaching in $13 Billion territory. Popular for drastically reducing the amount of time needed to ensure new transactions while ensuring more inclusive use of the coin, the Bitcoin alternative experiences a strong track record of loyal supporters around the world.

NEM

Gaining the nickname of "China's Ethereum," NEM is the digital currency popular for its proof-of-importance (POI) method rather than a proof-of-work (POW) system. In 2017, NEM grew 29,842%, three times as much as Ethereum, with a market cap of over $12.5 billion.

CAUSES OF THE ALTCOIN RALLIES
Bitcoin price

Bitcoin price is a crucial factor for the Altcoin price rally. "When Bitcoin's doing well, altcoins tend to follow that movement in price" (Chalmers). The same goes for when Bitcoin falls – altcoin prices will suffer as well. With capital pouring into Bitcoin after a bull run, investors and traders are beginning to turn their focus away to altcoins that may not yet have caught up.

Profits made from Bitcoin's bullishness tend to flow into the more prominent altcoins. This then blossoms from major altcoins into medium-cap coins, and then the smaller-cap coins, taking the whole cryptocurrencies market cap up.

While Bitcoin enjoyed enormous price gains during 2017, many altcoins outperformed it immensely. Sending many altcoins to the moon as it did not take much capital to see the underlying price of altcoins to rise and similarly it didn't take much capital to see the price of these altcoins to collapse.

FOMO

FOMO played a large part in altcoin rallies, especially in cryptocurrencies for first-time investors. Those new to cryptocurrencies often look at Bitcoin's price as it rises and think it has become too expensive, and they've missed the boat. Therefore, in the hopes that they can achieve what Bitcoin did and make them extremely wealthy, they look at the vastly cheaper Altcoins.

Bitcoin Dominance is a good indicator to reflect the above phenomenon. At the start of the bull run, Bitcoin's market dominance was above 90%, it soon saw a dramatic drop to below 60% from which it has not yet recovered till date as of 2020.

Altcoins like Ripple (XRP), NEM and Litecoin had seen astronomical price gains. But the secret to such massive gains, like other cryptocurrencies, is to make sure you sell while you're still in profit before they crash (as they typically do).

Pump-and-dump schemes

Although this is more common to a single altcoin than to the entire industry, there is still no solution to the issue of pump-and-dump schemes.

They were usually coordinated by social messaging

applications, such as Telegram, between a small group of people. They accumulate thinly traded coins at a low price, and dramatically pump the amount up, and then dump the coins for a profit shortly after that, causing the price to crash. Such schemes have been going on for many years, especially with illiquid altcoins, as they can be manipulated more easily.

Pumps and dumps resemble altcoin rallies, but they are much shorter. Those events usually take place over days or weeks, rather than months.

Conferences, new releases, announcements

Nothing stirs up altcoin fans like new releases or announcements. As these announcements build FOMO, people are rushing to buy up more coins in the hope of making a profit.

No cryptocurrency leader is as much of a hype-man as Justin Sun of Tron. Nobody does it better than him. He's able to keep the excitement buzzing around Tron through his marketing tactics to ensure his cryptocurrency doesn't lose any value.

As reported by Coin Rivet, Sun paid over $4 million for lunch with Warren Buffett, who has extremely negative opinions on cryptocurrencies. But, by doing this Sun ensured that Tron receives the appropriate press attention that highlighted his cryptocurrency, TRON, to audiences not familiar with the digital currency market.

CHAPTER THIRTEEN

THE FUTURE OF CRYPTOCURRENCIES POST-2020

It goes without saying that 2020 has been a tumultuous period across the globe. The growth, spread, and most recent mutation of the COVID-19 virus has resulted in a great deal of uncertainty in every sector—with the global economy hit particularly hard.

Western nations have struggled to create a unified, or even consistent plan to mitigate the spread of the disease, and measures taken to encourage economic activity have fluctuated wildly across region. In the U.S., State level responses have spanned the spectrum—from incredibly heavy-handed in the form of total shutdowns, to surprisingly relaxed in cases where local governing bodies have abstained from placing any punitive measures to support public health suggestions.

Such policy differences are separated not just geographically, but also temporally, with local policy makers changing health policy as the virus spreads. The market hates uncertainty, and 2020 has proven a solid example of this principle, with perhaps one exception.

Cryptocurrency and blockchain are exiting the year with a growing legacy of success, value, and mainstream adaptation. As of December 2020, Bitcoin has reached all-time highs with values over $20,000 per BTC—a substantial achievement after the major depreciation in 2018. For context, Bitcoin exited December of 2017 with a value of $19,783.06, but entered 2018 trading at around $13,500. That year, Bitcoin reached a low of $3,400. Similarly, another cryptocurrency Ethereum fell from $1,300 to $91 over the period of 2018 but rebounded to over $450 by December of 2020. A less substantial achievement, but still notable for a period of economic upheaval.

Blockchain has been meeting its own success in 2020, with an increasing number of institutions, investors, and mainstream enterprises showing interest. Larger investors mean increasingly larger trading volumes over those available to smaller, individual investors. An additional positive to this change is that, with such large institutions involved, the market will still be viable even with if there are less investors in total. Additionally, increased use means an increase in blockchain start-ups, and an increase in innovation. That said, the past year has managed to provide continual example of the technologies ability to meet the challenges of the new pandemic world.

As the Coronavirus continues, and a post-Covid world recedes further into the future with vaccine distribution falling increasingly behind projections—here are some predictions about how the world of blockchain and cryptocurrency will evolve in the coming months of 2021:

Investment Returns for Enterprise Blockchain

In the coming year, enterprise blockchain may continue to provide innovation and optimization for a multitude of business practices. For example, blockchain may assist in overcoming existing issues with consumer products, smart-city initiatives, and even minimizing supply chain disruptions outside of the Coronavirus context. If existing blockchain companies continue to work with larger corporations and government entities, and if those initiatives continue to display the potential of the technology—it is likely to lead to more blockchain startups entering the market.

If early pilot programs begin to show investment returns, this will also drive wider adaptation in the market, and thus continue to fuel innovation. We may see more insurance providers using blockchain technology to allow patients to access and share their medical data. Additionally, blockchain platforms may also allow content producers to manage and distribute their media to consumers without the need for a content delivery network.

Adaptation of Blockchain to further National Interests

Blockchain possesses significant abilities to track and log important financial information. Uses that include: sharing medical data, personal identity security, logistics monitoring, and even voting mechanisms.

In Asia, the technology is already being used to combat economic disruptions caused by the Coronavirus and to track financial payments related to the pandemic. In Singapore, large corporations are using blockchain technology to track supply-chain issues emerging as a result of the pandemic—and, in Japan, blockchain-based apps have been used to host shareholder meetings and allow for remote voting.

The success in these areas displays the real-world implications of blockchain use, and will likely encourage more widespread adaptation. Governments may see the benefit of using blockchain technology to track critical data related to Coronavirus and its spread, and such success would likely lead to further inter-governmental cooperation—using the technology to build a global network of information on the virus' spread and its detrimental effects.

The influx of movements for Public Banking

Another evolution in the economy potentially spurred on by the Coronavirus is public banking—a system that would allow its users to digitally store money, as well as transfer it to other users without a fee. Last year, there was a bill drafted by a group of New York politicians and lawmakers that would give digital wallets to all individuals and business in the states, and would allow them to make transactions using a statewide, public digital currency.

Similarly, a law now exists in California that allows municipalities to create public banks. While such a system would be incredibly beneficial to a society now practicing social distancing and engaging more and more with the economy online, the idea has failed to gain significant mainstream appeal. Still, the logic of its implementation is sound and if cryptocurrency continues to grow, lawmakers may continue to push for public banking solutions.

More legislative delays as Congress prioritizes the pandemic

Early last year saw the introduction of the Crypto-Currency Act of 2020 to congress. The purpose of the Act is described as follows within the document: "To clarify which Federal agencies regulate digital assets, to require those agencies to notify the public of any Federal licenses, certifications, or registrations required to create or trade in such assets, and for other purposes."

While this Act brings increased legislative attention to Federal involvement in Cryptocurrency, its path forward remains in limbo. The last action in congress regarding the Act was in March of 2020, where it was referred to the Committee on Financial Services, and Committee on Agriculture. No major news regarding the process has been disclosed since, and it is likely that the continued political turmoil in the U.S. will keep the legislative branch focused on COVID-19 related actions for some time.

Further use by Financial Institutions

As Cryptocurrency grows in strength, and we see more institutional involvement in the investment, it is likely that traditional financial service institutions will also begin to take notice. If 2021 sees a similar evolution as 2020, and if the global pandemic continues to present issues that cryptocurrency has the potential to mitigate, it is likely that cryptocurrencies will become more widely used by people in day-to-day life.

With luck, we may even begin to see its use in retail and mobile apps, as people look more and more to contactless alternatives for purchases. The use of cryptocurrency faces the same issue as all technologies, however. It relies on infrastructure to achieve wide use, but it needs wide use to justify investing in the infrastructure. While this may seem like a Catch-22, it is a hurdle that previous innovations like the credit card and diesel engine have overcome.

Even today, we see the rise of electric cars fueling the rise of charging stations. With cryptocurrency, its increased acceptance by financial institutions will only encourage more people to use it.

No significant changes to the prevalence of fraud

The year 2019 saw major growth in cryptocurrency crime, with the total value of losses doubling from the previous year to $4.5 billion. 2020 appears to have continued the trend of criminal innovation in the area of cybercrime.

In April of 2020, the Federal Bureau of Investigation predicted a rise in cryptocurrency related fraud schemes related to the Coronavirus. Similarly, in October of the same year Europol, the EU's law enforcement intelligence agency, released their Internet Organized Crime Threat Assessment.

This document stated that, "Indeed, the pandemic prompted significant change and criminal innovation in the area of cybercrime. Criminals devised both new modi operandi and adapted existing ones to exploit the situation, new attack vectors and new groups of victims."

As cryptocurrency continues to grow in purchasing power and popularity, so too will the number of individuals looking to take criminal advantage of it. Such a fact will likely bring further government scrutiny to the matter, and will likely result in some further specified legislation in the future.

Conclusion

While many of us are entering 2021 with understandable trepidation and uncertainty, it is worth looking forward towards the growth of cryptocurrency and blockchain technology, and the benefits it may have for a world growing increasingly contactless.

As our economies and supply-chains continue to weather pandemic related shocks, it is important that investors and institutions recognize the solutions afforded by growing blockchain innovations. Great administrative tasks, such as the vaccine rollout, are becoming increasingly more complex and difficult to organize, and it is important the potential of this technology is properly considered.

All that being said, both cryptocurrency and blockchain offer exciting areas for innovation and growth within the global financial system—their only true limitation is the willingness of people and institutions to make the jump. As we enter this new year, I am hopeful that their increased prevalence will accelerate their implementation in daily life.

REFERENCES

Brett King. The Biggest Threats To The Banking Sector, 2011,

http://www.finextra.com/blogs/fullblog.aspx?blogid=5945

Capital Market And International Business. URL:
https://2012books.lardbucket.org/books/challenges-and-opportunities-in-international-business/s11-02-understanding-international-ca.html

Chris Hoffman. Ethereum And Smart Contracts, 2018,
https://www.howtogeek.com/350322/what-is-ethereum-and-what-are-smart-contracts/

Cryptocurrency. URL: https://capital.com/crypto-market-news

Evan Weinberger, California Breathes New Life Into Public Banking Movement, 2021, https://news.bloomberglaw.com/banking-law/california-breathes-new-life-into-public-banking-movement

Federal Testimony. Fractional Reserve Banking, 2012, https://www.mercatus.org/publications/monetary-policy/fractional-reserve-banking

Fintech Futures. Top-performing altcoins in 2017, 2018, https://www.fintechfutures.com/2018/02/top-performing-altcoins-in-2017-fortune-jack/

Gertrude Chavez-Dreyfuss, Cryptocurrency Crime Losses More Than Double To $4.5 Billion in 2019, Report Finds, 2020, https://www.reuters.com/article/us-crypto-currencies-crime/cryptocurrency-crime-losses-more-than-double-to-45-billion-in-2019-report-finds-idUSKBN2051VT

History of Plastic money. URL:https://cashcofinancial.com/2016/01/the-history-of-plastic-money/

Ibrahim Rihan. *The Great Recession*. PDF. 2011

Jake Frankenfield. Bitcoin, 2020, https://www.investopedia.com/terms/b/bitcoin.asp

J. Singh. Money: Meaning and Functions of Money, 2012, https://www.economicsdiscussion.net/money/money-meaning-and-functions-of-money-discussed/597

Kimberly Amadeo. The 9 Principal Effects of the Great Depression, 2020, https://www.thebalance.com/effects-of-the-great-depression-4049299

Kimberly Amadeo. The History of the Gold Standard, 2020, https://www.thebalance.com/what-is-the-history-of-the-gold-standard-3306136

Ludvig von Mises Institute 2015, Criticism of the fractional reserve banking,

https://wiki.mises.org/wiki/Criticism_of_fractional_reserve_banking

Maria Valkonen. *Fractional Reserve in Banking System*. PDF. Haaga-Helia: University of Applied Science, 2016.

Money: Functions, Approaches, and Types. URL: https://www.economicsdiscussion.net/money-functions-approaches-and-types/4061

Money Definition. URL: https://boycewire.com/commodity-money-definition/

Nathan Reiff. Where Is The Cryptocurrency Industry Headed in 2021?, 2020, https://www.investopedia.com/where-are-cryptocurrencies-headed-2019-4580342

Paper Money. URL: https://www.investopedia.com/terms/p/paper_money.asp

Peter Knight. *Conspiracy Theories in American History*. PDF. 2003

Rep. Paul A Gosar, H.R.6154 – Crypto-Currency Act of 2020, 2020, https://www.congress.gov/bill/116th-congress/house-bill/6154/

Rose Chalmers. Causes of the Altcoin Rally, 2019, https://coinrivet.com/what-causes-an-altcoin-rally/

Supriya Guru. Paper Money: Convertible and Inconvertible, 2013, https://www.yourarticlelibrary.com/economics/money/paper-money-convertible-and-inconvertible-paper-money/37845

Stanley Finkelstein. *The Currency Act of 1764: A Quantitative Reappraisal.* Sage Publication, Inc., 1968.

Steve McNew. A 2020 And Post-Pandemic Outlook For Cryptocurrency And Blockchain Industries, 2020, https://www.forbes.com/sites/forbesbusinessdevelopmentcouncil/2020/05/21/a-2020-and-post-pandemic-outlook-for-cryptocurrency-and-blockchain-industries/#5580ddf763ab

Sarah Swammy et al. *Crypto Uncovered: The Evolution of Bitcoin and the CryptoCurrency Marketplace.* PDF. Palgrave Macmillan, 2018.

The Concise Oxford English Dictionary, 12th edition.

The Great Altcoin Bubble 2017. URL: https://www.financemagnates.com/cryptocurrencynewsbitcoin-and-icos-in-2017-a-year-in-review/

The History Of The Great Depression. URL: https://www.history.com/topics/great-depression/great-depression-history

Types of Money. URL: https://www.britannica.com/topic/money/Metallic-money

Valkonen Maria. *Fractional Reserve in Banking System.* PDF. Haaga-Helia: University of Applied Science, 2016.

www.ingramcontent.com/pod-product-compliance
Lightning Source LLC
Chambersburg PA
CBHW031929190326
41519CB00007B/460